KEN BEATTIE

TROWEL

Gardening Hints
from
Canada's Garden Guru

Trowel Tips

by
Ken Beattie

Second Printing — April 2003

Published by
Publishing Solutions/PW Group

Canadian Cataloguing in Publication Data

Beattie, Ken.

Trowel tips : gardening hints from Canada's garden guru

Includes index.
ISBN 1-894022-52-1

1. Gardening – Canada.   I. Title.

SB453.3.C2 B413   2000   635'.0971   C00-920156-4

Author Portrait by:
Don Hall,
Regina, Saskatchewan

Gardening Tools Photography by:
Patricia Holdsworth, Patricia Holdsworth Photography
Regina, Saskatchewan

Cover and Page Design by:
Brian Danchuk, Brian Danchuk Design
Regina, Saskatchewan

Page formatting and index by Iona Glabus

Designed, Printed and Produced in Canada by:
Centax Books, a Division of PW Group
Publishing Director: Margo Embury
1150 Eighth Avenue, Regina, Saskatchewan, Canada S4R 1C9
(306) 525-2304   FAX (306) 757-2439
E-mail: centax@printwest.com   www.centaxbooks.com

Table of Contents

Why Another Gardening Book? 4

Author, Author. 6

CHAPTER 1
Shady Characters & Sun Lovers 7

CHAPTER 2
Turf Trials & Tribulations 17

CHAPTER 3
Hankering for Herbs. 29

CHAPTER 4
Soil, Dirt 'n' Diggin'. 41

CHAPTER 5
Fungi, Bugs, Pestilence & Vermin 53

CHAPTER 6
Veggies, Fruit & Other Edibles 65

CHAPTER 7
Inside Out – Houseplants 81

CHAPTER 8
Propagation 95

CHAPTER 9
Bulbs, Corms, Rhizomes
   The Root of the Problem 111

CHAPTER 10
Maintenance, How To & Pruning. 125

Why Another Gardening Book?

Trowel Tips is not your average, everyday kind of gardening book. What kind of gardening book can this possibly be, for goodness sakes: the cover is white; there are no glossy color photos, the kind that make most of us drool; the print is large. Now there is a novel concept if ever I saw one. As I attempt to adjust to life with bifocals, I think that this is just a common courtesy to the reader and I do want the book to be easy to read and comfortable to hold.

Open it up and you'll discover that it is chock full of short snippets, all about the problems we all have in our gardens. Although not rocket science, I think you'll find this book a handy horticultural helper. Most of us have some difficulty admitting that we killed great Auntie Wendy's Christmas Cactus or even admitting to the fact that there are slugs in our Hosta patch. Nevertheless, we all have encountered a few (sometimes more than a few) problems in our gardens.

As I set about developing the manuscript for *Trowel Tips*, I looked back at the tens of thousands of questions people have asked me over the years. Attempting to satisfy all the query categories would make for a very fat text indeed, so I decided to reduce the content to ten chapters. These ten areas, I feel, address the most commonly asked gardening questions of our day. Each new topic is marked by a stylized green thumbprint to help you find your way.

Chapter One will have delights for gardeners in dappled light, partial shade and full sun. Shade has long been the nemesis of many a gardener, simply because it was so misunderstood. Actually, gardening with a limited amount of light can be very rewarding, indeed oodles of great plants prefer low light.

North Americans are obsessed with turf so I could not very well disregard the lawns of America in this book. Trials and Tribulations of Turf may help you perfect the technique or change your mind entirely about the common lawn.

Herbs, insects, vermin, pestilence, fruit and vegetables are discussed in the belly of the book, with a great deal of attention paid to houseplants in Chapter Seven. Wrapping up, I always like to assign a "to-do list", so Chapter Ten discusses maintenance, pruning and general chores for the gardener.

The text is written in common language and the content is practical. Where possible, I express a homemade remedy or practical tip that anyone can try without purchasing additional products. It is important to me that the information I pass on is not intimidating and can be easily followed. Let's face it, if the process is too complex or obscure, you are not likely to use it. I do not claim to be an organic gardener, however, where possible, I offer suggestions that will affect our environment to the minimum. Let's call it a common sense approach to the garden.

All in all, I hope that you find **Trowel Tips** a useful and entertaining little book. It is wise to never lose sight of the fact that a garden, no matter how big or small, mature or current, expensive or frugal, is always a work in progress. It is your garden and should be an extension of your soul, much like any other art form. Above all remember, if your garden is not as you wish this season, there is always next year.

Have fun, take time to enjoy your garden and share your knowledge.

Author, Author

Ken Beattie, one of Canada's favourite gardeners, shares his horticultural expertise with tens of thousands of avid gardeners each year through his television shows and personal presentations. Sometimes also creator and producer, he stars in three national television series, including *Get Growing* (a live call-in show with an audience reach of 5.8 million) and the international award-winning the *Earth's Garden*. Beattie has five more series and a four-part documentary film in production. In addition, he co-hosts, contributes and has guest appearances with several other national and international TV shows.

An engaging, enthusiastic and intelligent speaker, Beattie has presented on seven continents. During the frigid Canadian winters he regularly lectures aboard luxury cruise liners with exotic ports of call in South America, Africa, the Mediterranean and the South Pacific. A professional horticulturist for over 25 years, with 14 years of television experience, his presentations at horticultural shows range from Toronto's Canada Blooms, Vancouver's BC Home and Garden Show to Canadian Pacific Hotels' Gardener's Getaway Weekend series in Jasper and the University of Regina Environmental Education series.

Ken Beattie's new books, *Trowel Tips* and *Gardening Journal*, are packed with advice for the home gardener. They reflect his exuberant personality, witty style and years of gardening experience. Beattie's passion for and love of gardening are obvious in his books.

His goal is to help you garden more creatively, more successfully, and with more pleasure.

S
H A D Y
characters
&
sun lovers

7

Heuchera . . . Bless You!

☀ Heuchera, or Coral Bells, are delightful, hardy perennials. These low-growing, shade-tolerant plants come in a continuing variety of foliage patterns and floral colours. **Monet** is a creamy golden-foliaged new kid on the block for 2000. This variety, as all of them, tolerates alkaline conditions and prefers good drainage.

☀ Heuchera's close relative is the species Tiarella, often referred to as **Foam Flower**. Generally, these frothy white flowers are hardier than their cousins. Some cross breeding has occurred to develop the genus **"Heucherella"** which combines many of the positive attributes of both plants.

☀ Heuchera should be cleaned of dead foliage in the fall or first thing in the spring. As they are spreading in nature, caution should be exercised so as not to disturb newly forming crowns. I always feed them in the fall and again in the spring with bone meal.

☀ Some of the more exciting varieties of Heuchera are: **Can Can**, a grand display of closely ruffled claret purple leaves with silver splashes. **Mint Frost** has very clear silver blotching inlaid on minty green foliage. **Eco magnififolia** is superb, purple, green and silver married together on a huge leaf . . . striking!

☀ Companions to plant with Heuchera and Tiarella are Hosta for contrast, Japanese Iris for structure and vertical elements, and perhaps **Solomon's Seal** for graceful arching effects. These perennials require shade to semi-sun and like lots of moisture.

☀ The rampantly growing **Piggyback Plant** (*Tolmiea Menziesii*), a house plant, fits in perfectly with my shade-loving perennials. Why not? The leaves are so easily propagated and such a vivid green, they will enhance even the darkest nook in the garden. The point here is not to be bullied into thinking that you must only use plants that the garden centres and greenhouses have for sale as "bedding plants" or perennials.

Canna Lily . . . If It Wants To!

❉ Cannas make a wonderful addition to any sunny garden. They are a rhizomatous, tender perennial in most parts of North America, which means they should be lifted and stored indoors for the winter months. Generally, Cannas are started indoors in containers so they will be blooming before frost. Divide them in annually to increase inventory.

❉ In subtropical conditions, Cannas will grow the entire year, and grow they will. Their large, somewhat delicate leaves, will shade out anything that is attempting to grow at their base. Regular reductions in size often stimulate late season flowering.

❉ The tropical look is a popular garden theme either for decks and patios or balconies. Cannas lend themselves very well to containerization and provide a lush, tropical look. A rich soil, high in organic matter is preferred and I like to plant them in nothing smaller than a 14" (35 cm) container.

❉ Popular Canna varieties include: **Black Knight**, yellow and red **King Humbert**, **Orange Beauty**, **Primrose Yellow**, **Richard Wallace** and **Firebird**.

❉ Winter storage of Canna requires a considerable amount of room. The root mass generally is substantial as are the rhizomes themselves. Store them, cleaned of as much soil as possible, in dry Peat Moss or sawdust. It's a good idea to dust the rhizomes with an all-purpose fungicide/insecticide powder. Moist conditions encourage rot as do temperatures above 50°F (10°C).

❉ Canna are categorized, mainly by size, into three divisions. Semi-dwarf which reach 28 to 30" (70-90 cm), the mediums measuring in at 35 to 48" (90-20 cm) and tall at 48 to 60" (120-150 cm). A group of dwarf hybrids called **Pfitzer Cannas** reach 24 to 30" (60-70 cm).

In The Dark About Shade?

☀ Plants which tolerate full sun and are often drought tolerate, too, have a greyish foliage. This silvery foliage can reflect some of the sun's energy rather than allowing it to bake the plant.

☀ Knowing where a plant grows naturally is often a benefit. Attempting to grow a marsh-loving plant in full sun can be done, but not easily. Look for plants that are native to Africa, south-western America and alpine areas. Most of these plants will have a natural tolerance to full sun.

☀ **Mulching** is a great benefit to plants grown in full sun. The layer of organic or inorganic material will keep the soil at a more moderate temperature as well as maintain better moisture levels. Mulch is not necessarily considered a permanent item, the plant itself will eventually cover the area and form a **living mulch**.

☀ Shade and perennials are two words that gardeners would like to see together more often. One good old standby is Hosta, of course, and the attractive Bugbane will turn a few eyes also. Hellebores delight gardeners in early spring with their pastel shades against greening grass.

☀ A great deal of garden literature will state hardiness zones from either USDA or Canadian Department of Agriculture information. Naturally, those businesses which guarantee plant hardiness will err on the side of safety and list the plants in zones much higher than they might be able to grow in. Heuchera is a prime example, listed as hardy to USDA zone 4. I have grown them for years in a zone 2.

☀ One of my newest favourites to the shade garden is *Brunnera macrophylla*. Often called Siberian Bugloss, the variegated form is much nicer than the name might imply. I grow my specimens in full shade and with oodles of water in a rich woodland soil. They perform flawlessly each season and add a striking compliment of blue to your garden.

Anatomically Correct

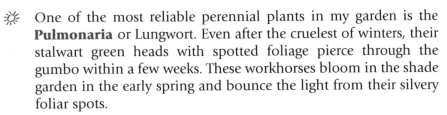

※ One of the most reliable perennial plants in my garden is the **Pulmonaria** or Lungwort. Even after the cruelest of winters, their stalwart green heads with spotted foliage pierce through the gumbo within a few weeks. These workhorses bloom in the shade garden in the early spring and bounce the light from their silvery foliar spots.

※ What's in a name anyway – Lungwort . . . what is up with this? Actually, wort is an old English name for herb. The lung aspect comes from early apothecaries who believed the spotted leaves looked like lungs. This attribute, and I think the time of year that the plant is in bloom, springtime . . . gave rise to the notion that Pulmonaria could heal lung problems. Spring is also cold and pneumonia season for many maritime climates.

※ I remember these plants from my childhood. They peered out, first and brave, under the Lilac shrubs near the garage. Curious things I remember thinking, spotted leaves and two-toned flowers, pink and blue on the same plant. As any kid would do, I picked a bouquet to bring indoors, only to learn that they are better out-doors as they are very short lived.

※ Pulmonaria are excellent companions with Hosta, Tiarella, Heuchera and Epimedium. The varieties with brighter leaves such as **Excalibur** brighten up even the dullest corner of the shade garden. **Silver Streamers** is another tremendous variety, sporting long, ruffled, near pure silver leaves.

※ Bethlehem Sage is the common name for ***Pulmonaria saccharata***. This low-maintenance group of lungworts sport the most silver in their larger leaves. ***Pulmonaria longifolia*** brings strap-shaped narrow leaves to the gene pool. Mix and match no matter what the name, they all take a wonderful family photo.

※ Propagation of Lungwort is very easily accomplished. I divide mine, rather ruthlessly, in the early spring either before bloom or just after, depending on the amount of rain. They tend to grow in clumps that lend themselves to division. Neighbours and other gardeners will line up to exchange with you.

※ The shade-loving perennial **Lungwort** should have its foliage trimmed back in June. This encourages a great flush of new foliage and allows neighbouring plants to enjoy some extra light.

☀ Lungworts should be cut back in the autumn as they get rather sprawling. I mark the area so as not to overplant them with new treasures.

☀ Hostas are shade-loving plants with large, coarse, decorative foliage. These plants prefer a consistently moist, rich soil. Unfortunately, these conditions are ideal for slugs. One "slug resistant" Hosta is called **Sum and Substance**. Well worth a try.

☀ Dry shade is a difficult condition in which to coax anything to thrive. I have found at least one plant that looks promising, Joe Pye Weed, but not the meadow variety that slurps up water, ***Eupatorium rugosum* 'Chocolate'**. A super colour and tolerant of poor conditions, this is a sturdy, easy-to-grow specimen.

☀ The definitions of sun and shade and all the degrees between can be very confusing. By my definition, deep shade areas receive less than two hours of direct light per day. Full sun, receives direct light for more than four hours per day. Semi, partial, indirect and other adjectives describe the intensities in-between.

☀ Too much sun, particularly on balcony gardens, can be overcome with strategically placed plants. Consider planting a large container of Scarlet Runner Beans and prepare a trellis of string or wire for them to climb. They will easily fill in the balcony expanse. Once these botanical shades are up, plant anything behind that tolerates lower light. To increase light, simply prune the Beans.

Fern Gully

☀ Nothing says shade better than Ferns. Even in the coldest portions of the country there are Ferns that will survive. **Ostrich Ferns** range from zone 1 through zone 9. Remember to keep the area moist and rich, woodland soil is best. I have never had great success with these Ferns in containers, but more tropical varieties do well.

☀ Maidenhair Ferns or ***Adiantum pedatum*** appear to be tropical. Don't let their fragile appearance fool you, they are great in the bog or woodland garden. I enhance the soil with lots of compost and Peat Moss, to hold moisture and acidify the area slightly. They lose their foliage for the winter but, with a good mulch of dry leaves, they will survive even a northern blizzard.

Pleasantly Predictable Peonies

☼ Peonies do not like a great deal of fertilizer. As a matter of fact, if they are on too heavy a diet, they will not bloom. A good cultural regime is to apply bone meal in the spring and then leave them alone for the season.

☼ Peonies are well suited for the cooler regions of North America, with a few exceptions and specialties for the warmer south. They require a cold period of dormancy in order to set flower for the following year. **Zones 2 through 7** have the best success with these stately perennials. They prefer a sunny location.

☼ Peonies will not bloom if the growing tip or eyes are planted too deeply. Generally, they should be 2" (5 cm) below soil level. Heat waves and early summer temperatures will throw Peonies off schedule also. There is not much that can be done to remedy this, but . . . there is always next year!

☼ Fernleafed Peonies are unusual looking and treasured by most. *Paeonia tenuifolia 'Rubra Plena'* is a gorgeous deep-red double Fernleaf. Unlike most of the gang, this one prefers to be kept a little on the dry side. One grower suggests that the roots be planted on a slight angle to accomplish this. As with all Peonies, the spent blossoms should be removed.

☼ **Ants are important to the culture of Peonies** . . . aren't they? One sure would think so as there are generally millions of ants around when the buds are formed. I think that the ants are after the sticky substance that encases the bud sheath, and continue to clean it off until the buds open. Maybe the buds would never open if the ants didn't help!

☼ In the Ottawa region of Ontario, Canada, Peonies bloom about the first week of June. This coincides perfectly with many small town "Decoration Sundays" in local church yards and cemeteries. This ritual in my hometown became a good substitute for a non-juried floral show. This was a surefire way of seeing the finest flowers the town had grown, all in one location.

Sun Worship

☼ *Mina lobata* or *Quamoclit lobata* will produce hundreds and hundreds of elongated, tubular flowers. What I find interesting about these self-twining plants is their ability to change colour as the flowers age. Starting out a rich red, they progress to orange, through yellow and eventually white. For those of us that have difficulty making up our minds, a perfect specimen. I would grow this plant with protection from the wind and treat it as an annual.

☼ One of the easiest and brightest coloured flowers to grow in full sun is **Portulaca**. This mighty annual almost seems to prefer a location near pavement, concrete or other heat-attracting material. It has a close cousin, the **Mesembryanthemums**, from Africa. These juicy-leafed annuals appear as if they have been dusted with confectioners' sugar. They too enjoy full, hot sun and erupt in brightly coloured flowers all season long.

☼ Sunflowers are a wonderful plant to excite children and introduce non-gardeners to the joys of this lifestyle. Easily grown from seed, these rewarding beauties range in size and colour from dwarf **Teddy Bears** to mammoth **Russian Giants**, red, pink, terra cotta and exotics. Start them indoors in early May and transplant outdoors for truly spectacular results. As their name implies, these plants are sun loving.

☼ Evening Primrose or *Oenothera odorata*, are delightful "back-of-the-border" plants. The flowers of this sun lover are attractive at all stages of development from bud to seed head. Their delicate scent is more noticeable in the evening.

☼ *Nicotiana X sanderae* or Flowering Nicotine has a powerful fragrance in the early evening. This all-time favourite is easily grown in the sunny border or large containers. Dwarf varieties are suitable for window boxes and mixed plantings. Whatever the size, the aroma is always huge.

☼ Tomatoes and Green Peppers are excellent sun-loving, container plants. I grow Roma Tomatoes in a large, terra cotta planter. My preference for terra cotta is more than just aesthetic, it has a foundation in physics. Terra cotta breaths, so the roots and soil do not stagnate. Also, the colour of terra cotta and the density are excellent for attracting and holding heat.

☼ The sun can be a very **reliable weed killer**. Lay a sheet of high-grade black plastic over the area infested with weeds. Let the sun beat down on this plastic sheet for two or three weeks. The soil underneath will bake and kill out almost all of the weeds.

☼ Sun-drying or curing Onions is the best method in my opinion. In the late summer, after the tops of the Onions have been bent down, lift the bulbs. I like to remove as much soil as I can, then lay them in the sun, stalks intact, to dry. The warm autumn days cure the Onions so that they keep well over the winter. A well-ventilated bag is the best way to store Onions in cool storage.

☼ The Sunflower farm that I have planned for this year's garden includes four special kinds. **Taiyo**, which grows about 6' (1.8 m), is a golden yellow, large-headed variety. The other three are between 5' (1.5 m) and 6' (1.8 m) tall with great colours. **Evening Sun** and **Velvet Queen** are mahogany shades to velvety crimson. To set off the whole works, I have **Lemon Queen,** a very early-blooming clear-yellow variety.

☼ *Echinops ritro* or the Globe Thistle, is one of the coolest plants in the sunny perennial border. Its metallic-blue colour is only exceeded by the bizarre-looking "spiked golfball" flowers. Put this prize at the rear of the border and expect comments. I like to grow it in rich, well-drained soil, this way the spiked spheres get even larger. Try it with baby's breath for contrast.

☼ Delphiniums are so stately and bold in the sunny perennial border. They should be staked early on in the season to avoid "windy disappointments". Rich moist but well-drained soil is imperative for huge floral spikes. **Rotenone**® is also a good idea. The Larkspur Worm can devour a developing flower stalk overnight. This product is dusted on and is the only one that I have found to be effective.

☼ I recall my childhood neighbour's garden as the home of a giant **Golden Glow**. As a kid, I only knew that this monstrous plant developed huge, yellow, Chrysanthemum-like flowers and always was three times my height. As it turns out, this Rudbeckia variety is still available today but dwarf progenies are more popular. It was once referred to as the "outhouse plant".

Sunny Borders

☀ Gloriosa Daisy, Rudbeckia or the Black-Eyed Susan of our childhood are tremendous sun lovers. Superb for cutting and drying, these workhorses of the perennial garden should not be overlooked. Try the dainty **Rudbeckia maxima**, whose tall, chocolate cone is predominant. The foliage is "blue" and is almost as attractive as the flowers. Native to North America, it is easily grown.

☀ Scabiosa is a horrid name for anything, particularly something as nice as this sun-loving perennial. I grow these Pincushion Flowers in profusion in the sunniest portion of my Rose garden. Their stately, azure-blue flowers contrast beautifully with my pink Roses. The more you cut the flowers of **Scabious**, the more they seem to produce. If all this isn't enough, they also attract butterflies.

☀ **Hemerocallis** or Daylilies were, for the longest time, the outcasts of many gardens. Perhaps it was the old orange varieties that grew along abandoned farmsteads that gave them the bad image I, for one, think they are great. Today there are hundreds of new hybrids with almost every colour of the rainbow. They love sun, water and require little maintenance. What's bad about that?

☀ Mullein or **Verbascum** is one of the finest perennials for the sunny cottage garden. Beware, once you have one you will always have Verbascum, they seed profusely. The variety I grow, **V. Chiaxii 'alba',** has come to be know as "Ken's plant" to the neighbours. It is white with a super carmine eye in each flower. Try them, they are easy from seed and the neighbours love them.

☀ The grasses are playing an ever-increasing role in the sunny border and landscapes. I am not a particular fan, perhaps I have weeded too much Quack in my day! At any rate **Helictotrichon sempervirens** (Blue Oat Grass) makes a dandy addition to the garden.

☀ St. John's Wort is popular in herbal remedies and in the sunny corners of a garden. If you have a difficult slope to retain or steep embankments, **Hypericum calycinum** is great. It is non-specific for soil type and will endure some drought. I have always been fond of its rich yellow flowers throughout the season.

☀ Penstemons, or Beard's Tongue, never did a whole lot for me, but I have lots of sun in one large perennial bed and am always looking for variety. The **Penstemon digitalis 'Husker Red'** jumped out at me at a local garden centre. Now I love this plant with its dark, sultry foliage and rampant growth. Good drainage is the key.

T U R F
trials
&
tribulations

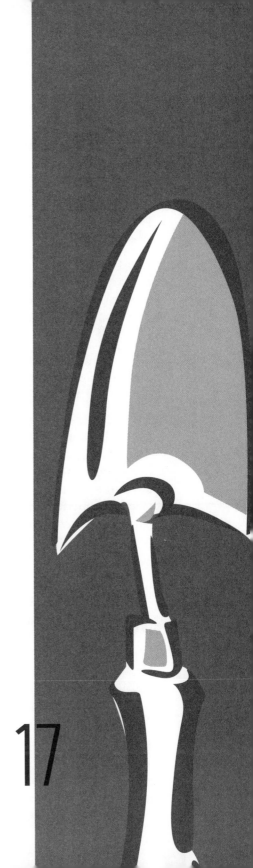

17

The Skinny on Turf Diets

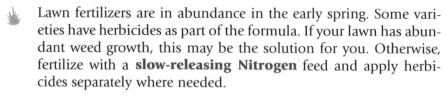

- Lawn fertilizers are in abundance in the early spring. Some varieties have herbicides as part of the formula. If your lawn has abundant weed growth, this may be the solution for you. Otherwise, fertilize with a **slow-releasing Nitrogen** feed and apply herbicides separately where needed.

- Turf grass will benefit from a liberal addition of fertilizer in August. I like to use a granular product that has a higher ratio of Phosphorus and reduced Nitrogen. A feed such as this encourages strong root growth.

- Ammonium nitrate is a great fertilizer if you have lots of water and a sharpened lawnmower blade. Curiously enough, it is also a component in some explosives . . . I wonder if there is a connection.

- Nitrogen is the first element in a fertilizer ratio, followed by Phosphorus then Potassium. Good turf requires some of each of these elements to promote strong, healthy growth. Nutrients can be derived from organic and inorganic sources.

- Should you leave **grass clippings** on the lawn or gather them using the bagger attachment of the lawn mower? Generally, in drier climates, such as on the Prairies, grass clippings do not decompose rapidly and therefore should be picked up. Mulching lawnmowers are ideal for incorporating clippings back into the lawn. Frequent cutting results in smaller amounts of clippings which can be mulched back into the lawn even in the driest regions of the country.

Water Wise for Turf

- During summer months approximately 50% of all treated water is applied to Canadian lawns. Between 1972 and 1991 Canada's water withdrawal increased by 80%, the population only grew by 3%

- Turf is, without doubt, the thirstiest mono culture grown in North America. If you are attempting to conserve water in your gardening region, you may consider reducing the amount of turf that you maintain.

Irrigation systems are as varied as the gardeners that use them. From the watering can to automatic systems, a few basic notions are considered. Apply water in the early part of the day to allow plants time to dry before nightfall. This habit will reduce the amount of fungal-related problems.

 Do you have a soaker hose? You know the flat kind that is punctured with tiny pin-hole-sized openings . . . it pees everywhere, you know . . . ! Well, let's put that in the trash can. This waste of water is perhaps the most efficient way to make clouds. If you can't bring yourself to discard it, at least turn it over so the water sprays down and not into the air.

 On a warm July day, with a light breeze blowing, up to **70%** of the water that squirts through the irrigation nozzle **evaporates**. That's a lot of clouds! With equipment that maintains a lower projectile angle of water evaporation is somewhat reduced.

 The recommended amount of water for the average North American lawn is 1" (2.5 cm) per week. How do you measure that? Simply place a rectangular cake pan (9 x 13"/23 x 33 cm) on the area to be irrigated. Turn the system on and time how long it takes to fill the pan. This roughly approximates 1" (2.5 cm) of water. Generally, it will take about 60 minutes.

Fungus Among Us

 Snow mould is characterized by the telltale black slimy appearance of the turf. The disease tends to form in circular patterns and almost always follows a winter with lingering snow and excessive water during the runoff. Golf courses and public green spaces will most likely combat the problem chemically, as their livelihood and reputation may depend on how the turf looks. I am approaching the problem with less intervention. I suggest that the homeowner concerned with turf fungal ailments remove the snow from the turf as soon as possible.

 Powdery Mildew is prevalent on a great many lawns in late spring and early summer. Cooler temperatures and moisture from heavy dew and autumn rains encourage this blight to spread. Unless you own a golf course, I would suggest that you trim the lawn regularly, discard the clippings and **forget fungicide applications**.

Lawn Laws

Spring trims of turf are not as critical as at other times of the year. It is this season that turf is actively growing after a long winter's rest. I use an electric lawn mower that catches the trimmings rather than mulching them back into the turf. The **setting** of the lawn mower can be **lower in the spring** than in the summertime. I use the second notch which gives me about 1½" (4 cm) of turf blade when trimmed. The reason that I do not mulch the leaf blades back down is because I have a very dry summer, as a rule, and the trimmings take considerable time to mulch. If you have a mulching lawn mower, and your summer is also dry, consider cutting the turf more often so that the trimmings are smaller. This way they will decompose and add some nutrient back to the turf.

Edging is the term given to removing a thin slice of turf at the border of a flower bed or soil area. I can recall edging what seemed to be miles of manicured flower beds in the Niagara Parks Commission. We were sent out with a sharpened **half-moon edger**, a metal file and a good hat. The edger was regularly sharpened so the razor-thin slices could be removed without tearing the turf. Our mentors did all but use micrometers to ensure our edges were perfectly formed. On a clay soil, the edges can be almost vertical; on sandy or light soils, anywhere from 45 degree angles and less. The function is not strictly aesthetic, this sharp edge also inhibits turf grass from growing into the beds.

Heavy traffic areas on turf grass or lawns which are struggling on clay soils, or are over 10 years old, should be **aerated** in the fall. Choose the equipment that removes the soil core rather than those which simply perforate. Remove the castings and apply a top-dressing of clean, high-grade topsoil. This process should be repeated in the spring.

Rolling a lawn area is common practice on playing fields and lighter soils. Clay soils do not enjoy a good rolling as it actually compacts the soil too much, and the turf will suffer. Rolling is accomplished by dragging a water-filled or, in some cases, concrete drum over moist turf. The notion is to smooth out any frost heaves and other "disfiguring" marks of winter. Generally, rolling is one of the first chores of the spring.

Topdressing a turf grass area is a very common practice in North America. No matter how careful a person is, turf will suffer from the winter weather. Bare patches and thinning areas need to be addressed very early in the spring. Top dressing is the application of a very good topsoil and manure mix to the bare patches. I use the backside of a hard rake to smooth any lumps and spread the soil. It is applied so that the existing turf is still visible through the new soil. Often, greenskeepers will add a high-Phosphorus fertilizer to encourage the turf to root into this new soil. In severe cases seed is applied, too.

Thinning Out – A Lawn In Crisis!

 Varieties of turf commonly used in our lawns have different appearances. **Fescue**, the turf that is most commonly used in shade mixes, has a very thin leaf blade. **Blue Grasses**, in all of their various varieties, have a considerably broader leaf blade. If you have sown a "mixed" grass seed plot, and the area is more shady than sunny, chances are the area will thin out as the blue grasses die out. **Nurse grasses** are sometimes included in mixes as well. The most popular is Rye Grass. It germinates early and provides shade for the developing turf grasses. The nurse crop often dies out after the first season.

 Seed versus sod is an age-old debate. Personally, I prefer to sod a lawn area. The preparation of the soil bed is very similar for both, but sod gives immediate satisfaction. Seeded lawns are great for a single species grass or specific mix for a specific purpose. Golf courses, lawn bowling greens and high-use turf are often seeded. My experience has been that I provide the birds with a very expensive buffet.

 Turf grass germinates very well in cool spring weather. I have seen areas sown on top of the first skiff of autumn snow or late in the spring. This is actually not a bad idea, you at least can see how thickly you are sowing and as the snow melts it provides immediate water. The **water is the key** to good germination. Seed will sit dormant in cool weather until there is sufficient moisture.

Plugs of sod are a fast way to fill in a thinning lawn. If you are edging the lawn area or removing sod for a new flower bed, save the trimmings. I use these as "plugs" or transplants in the bare spots. Simply cultivate the soil, dig a small hole and insert the plug of sod. Water is crucial to development as is a bit of high-Phosphorus fertilizer.

 Reasons for a thinning lawn are varied. Pets are the most common ailments, followed by age. **Older lawns**, particularly those subject to heavy foot traffic, wear out rapidly if they are not maintained. In public areas, I have seen large expanses cordoned off to prevent traffic until the thinning sod can be **topdressed, seeded or resodded**. If at all possible, redirect traffic on your turf area throughout the growing season to avoid wear and tear damage. Golf courses do this as a matter of daily maintenance, so why not at home?

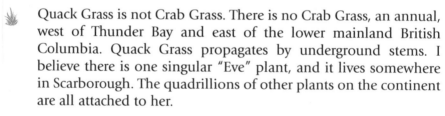

Unwanted Intruders – non-legged

 Quack Grass is not Crab Grass. There is no Crab Grass, an annual, west of Thunder Bay and east of the lower mainland British Columbia. Quack Grass propagates by underground stems. I believe there is one singular "Eve" plant, and it lives somewhere in Scarborough. The quadrillions of other plants on the continent are all attached to her.

 Crab Grass can be effectively controlled with a chemical product called Dacthal®. Although the plant is green and resembles grass, true turf types find it as disgusting as a bathtub ring in a hotel tub. I am just glad that this is one plant I don't have to be concerned with.

Dandelions and flowering broad-leafed weeds are the bane of many a gardener. In some regions of North America, there are movements to **ban the use of herbicides**. Whether this is good or bad matters not, the dandelions will still be around. If you plan on using a herbicide to control broad-leafed, perennial weeds, the best time to apply is in the fall. The dandelions and thistles are storing nutrients for the winter in their tap roots. Applications of herbicides travel into the roots as well, killing the plants rather quickly.

Creeping Charlie is the name given to the plant *Glecoma heder-aceae*. Personally, I think it is a very attractive vine with potential in other parts of the garden, not the lawn. Charlie is most happy in a shady, moist nook of the lawn, so that his roots are cool. The vine has opposite pairs of roundish leaves which root at each node. This action, akin to how a strawberry roots, makes Charlie a particularly difficult turf weed to eradicate. Some gardeners apply **2,4-D**® with an extra drop of insecticidal or dishwashing soap added. The thinking is that the soap will help the product stick to Charlie's leaves.

 Thistles are not the easiest turf weeds to eradicate. The most effective method is to dig them out after soaking the area with water. You may not realize that if a portion of a thistle stem remains in the soil, as a result of you pulling and breaking it off, it will grow again. This is why soaking the area is a good idea, it softens the soil so that the roots will pull more easily. Fall applications of non-selective herbicides directly to the thistles also work well.

 Non-Selective herbicides, **Glyphosinate ammonium** to be precise, must react with chlorophyll to be effective. This family of herbicides does not contaminate the soil and is generally used across the continent. However, be sure of your aim, all things green are targets, even your jeans.

Unwanted Intruders – legged

 Skunks, as unpleasant as they are, do not dig up turf for any other reason than to find dinner. Larvae of many beetles are soil borne and the favourite snack for the skunk. So, to discourage smelly, nocturnal visits, treat the soil to get rid of the grubs. **Chlorisect**® is a popular brand name of a chemical designed for this purpose. Drenching with soapy water in the area where the grubs are heavy will also slow them down.

 Sod webworm in a lawn is characterized by brown rings, usually in July. These critters are small, grub-like larvae with dark-coloured heads. It doesn't really matter what they look like, their appetites are what are the problem. They munch away on the root hairs of the turf, causing the plants to die, hence the brown rings. The heaviest concentration of **web worm** larvae are at the "frontier" of green turf and brown turf. Drenching these zones with a strong solution of insecticidal soap will slow down the activities, or use a drench of **Diazinon**®.

Chinch bugs are prevalent on Prairie lawns. These characters are similar to webworm only they are usually earlier in the season. A lawn that is very moist is the favourite home for chinch bugs. There are several species of this insect, all with specific tastes for turf. Aeration and keeping the sod in excellent growing condition helps to combat chinch bugs. A drench of **insecticidal soap** will also reduce their numbers. In some areas milky spore is available. This product is a natural predator of the larvae as are certain nematodes. If you wish to use pesticides, **Pyrethrums** are recommended.

 Ants are numerous and can really damage the appearance of a lawn. Sandier and lighter soils are the preferred sites for ants but they will live anywhere that is not too moist. This fact is one of the methods of encouraging ants to leave the lawn, soak them out. Unfortunately, the ants just move to another location and set up shop. Boiling water is very effective against ants, but be careful not to spill the water on the turf, it will kill it, too. Ants often will build their nests close to turf areas and concrete walks. Use the hot water on the paving. **Borax** will also control ants but is toxic to plants in large quantities.

 Worms in the garden are a very good sign. (Yes, I know that they don't have legs, but they seemed to fit into this section nicely.) Many people attempt to eradicate worms from turf and vegetable gardens, not realizing the benefits that they provide. To encourage worms, the soil requires ample organic matter, moisture and a peaceful environment. Perhaps the rototiller should spend more time in the shed.

 Dog spots on the lawn are among the least attractive signs of spring. One method that I use with fairly good results incorporates agricultural lime or gypsum. This is sprinkled on the damaged area after the dead grass is removed. Ample water is applied to soak in the powder and **neutralize the acid** and acrid soil. If the area is larger than a paint can, I plant sod plugs acquired from the day's edging. Smaller areas can be reseeded or left to fill in on their own.

Odds and Sods

Preparations **for sodding a new lawn** are where one should spend most of the effort. It is not just a matter of scratching the surface of the soil, slapping the sod down, watering and presto! The soil should be either tilled or cultivated to afford drainage and amended to incorporate organic matter to hold moisture. Topsoil to a depth of 6" (15 cm) is often also recommended. I like to apply a granular fertilizer with high Phosphorus and mix it in prior to laying the sod. Some folks like to roll the topsoil to ensure that all the air pockets are eliminated. Not a bad idea as roots which come in contact with air will dry and die rapidly.

Sod comes in two basic types, one is soil based, the other is peat based. I am not fond of **peat-based** varieties at all. Peat, as you may be aware, holds a great deal of moisture, this is a good thing. Dry peat however, is very difficult to moisten. Sod grown on peat which has been kept moist will perform well if the soil that it is placed on is of similar tilth. My experience has been that, even after several years, peat-based sod can be rolled up as the roots remained in the peat and did not penetrate into the subsoil.

Knitting is a technique which is applied when sod is being installed. The seams of the sod should be offset much like laying tiles. The edges of each piece of sod are lifted above the soil slightly, matched and then forced down into the soil. This knitting relieves any shrinkage gaps after the sod is laid. Some people actually overlap the sod edges to achieve the same end. I find that this leaves an uneven surface and is less desirable.

Immediate maintenance, once the sod is down, is to **water**. The second most important function is to **water** and, finally, **water** again. Assuming that you applied a granular fertilizer to the sub soil, there is no need to fertilize the new sod. Watering is particularly crucial if the day is warm and windy.

Slopes can be sodded successfully if you use pegs to hold the sod in place. It is a good idea to paint the tops of the pegs a bright colour so you can see them, or the first time you cut the new lawn the pegs may end up in the lawnmower. **Stabilizing the slope** with chicken wire is sometimes done, also. The wire is attached with large wire staples or pegs and the sod draped over it and pegged as well. Ideally, steep slopes should be seeded, if possible.

Seeding a New Lawn

Preparing a seed bed for a lawn is a **great deal of work**. The sub-soil should be well cultivated and, if it is clay, broken up to provide drainage. Triple Mix® or other high-grade topsoil is applied to a depth of at least 6" (15 cm) and then raked smooth. Slope and contour for the lawn are established and extra organic matter is added and raked in. The seed is broadcast either using a mechanical spreader or by hand. Water is applied, settling the seed into the soil. A lot of gardeners will cover the area (if it is small) with burlap. This keeps the birds out of the seed and provides some shade for the seed to germinate.

I have never sown a single-species lawn, always using a mixture of grasses and nurse crop. My reluctance may be because I am not a turf lover in the first place and a single-species lawn might be more work for me. I have seen some beautiful lawns, manicured to within an inch of their lives, and just waiting for a flag and cup. **My lawns are purely functional** (dog and kids) and, I think, typical of most Canadian lawns.

Newly sown lawn areas should be cordoned off and well marked. There is nothing more frustrating than someone's big number 10s on your new lawn. It seems that the seed still germinates in the imprint, leaving a curious look at best. **Birds are also a problem**. The grass seed is sown at a time in the spring when there is not a lot for them to eat. Aluminum pie pans, surveyors' tape and general activity around the area will help keep the winged munchers at bay.

The **first cutting** of the seeded lawn should be once the soil has settled and the seedlings are turning a dark green. Soft seedlings can be pulled out with the vacuum effect of the lawn mower. Ensure that the blade of the **mower is very sharp** and adjust the height to just trim the tops of the turf. I suggest that, if possible, you allow the trimmings to stay on the new lawn. They will provide mulch, shade and retain soil moisture.

Ornamental Grasses

Ornamental grasses have taken the North American landscape by storm. During the late 90s a person could find varieties and species of grasses that would suit every taste, persuasion and location. From the vivid blues of **Fescue** to the fuzzy flowers of the fountain grasses, all are graceful. I am more fond of the clumping grasses or mounds, such as **Blue Oat Grass**, as they tend to stay somewhat in check.

Hardiness is a concern for many gardeners when it comes to ornamental grasses. A few are hardy to Canadian Department of Agriculture zone 2, like *Arrhenatherum bulbosum* **'Oat Grass'** and *Phalaris arundinacea* **'Ribbon Grass'**. The majority of these grand grasses are hardy to zone 4, with a few only hardy in zone 9. As **zones are only guidelines**, check with your local garden centre or horticultural society, people there may have grown some out-of-range grasses with good success.

Perennial grasses are those which are supposed to live through at least one winter. **Containerized grasses**, if not in the very mildest of conditions, will not winter very well. Snow cover will extend the hardiness range of many grasses as will ample moisture in the fall. If you have access to a cool garage, store the potted grasses in there for the winter.

Blue tones are the most popular in plants and the ornamental grasses are no exception. *Andropogon scoparius* **'The Blues'** is bred from a native North American grass that once covered most of the Prairies. This is a clumping grass, like so many native species, that is well suited for large naturalization projects. It is rather drought tolerant and will perform well on alkaline soils.

To Bed – The Season Ends

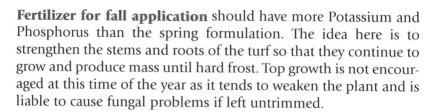

🌱 **Fertilizer for fall application** should have more Potassium and Phosphorus than the spring formulation. The idea here is to strengthen the stems and roots of the turf so that they continue to grow and produce mass until hard frost. Top growth is not encouraged at this time of the year as it tends to weaken the plant and is liable to cause fungal problems if left untrimmed.

🌱 The final cutting of the lawn marks a milestone in the annual history of the garden. I, for one, am glad that this point has arrived. The turf should be **cut fairly short for the last time** and the clippings removed either by hand raking or using the catcher on the mower. Leaving debris and long grass encourages fungal problems and in some cases, animals. Voles are small rodents which occur in large numbers on the Prairies. Long turf provides them with a wonderful refuge for the winter. They scramble along under the snow on "runways" under the long grasses. In the spring, there are hundreds of racetracks of damaged turf.

🌱 **Bulb planting in turf** areas can provide an interesting show for the following season. Crocus are the most commonly naturalized bulbs in turf. One way to plant these is throw the tiny bulbs up in the air and where they land on the sod, plant them. This eliminates any military precision. The bulbs push through the spring turf with little effort. One drawback is that the foliage should be left until the second or third cutting. This is not acceptable to some turf aficionados.

🌱 Cat Grass is very easy to grow indoors. Actually, I think that it is plain old oats, but it sells better if it is called **Cat Grass**. Obtain a suitable container to hold soil, preferably with drainage. Fill the container with a porous potting medium and moisten it down. Plant the seeds on the surface and press them into the moist soil. Germinate on the refrigerator for about a day. The bottom heat from the fridge really speeds the process along. Once the seeds are up and you can see green, place the container in good light and enjoy. Even if there is no cat in the house, the plants make a great addition to any room.

HANKERING
for herbs

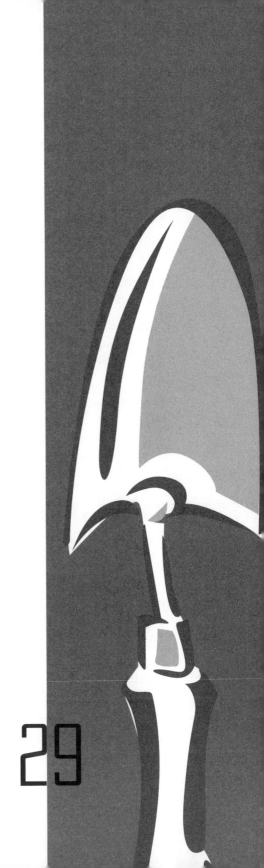

Basic Basil-ese

- Basil is one of the most popular herbs grown in North American gardens. Unfortunately, many varieties suffer from a nasty "Fusaium oxysporum" fungus. One Basil that is not only excellent in pesto but is disease resistant is the Genovese variety **Nufar**.

- Basil grows very well in North American gardens, provided the soil is warm and fertile. Never plant Basil into early spring soil that has not been warmed up. Try laying a sheet of black poly over the intended planting area a few weeks prior. The sun will heat the plastic and thus the soil underneath, providing an excellent hot spot for the crop.

- Apparently the Greek word for king – **basileus**, is the genesis for the royal herb Basil.

- Storing the year's harvest of Basil is best accomplished as pesto, in my opinion. Although this herb can be dried, stored in oil, or frozen fresh, the flavour is altered considerably.

- Walkways are always enhanced if the plants along the edge, within brushing distance as a person walks by, are highly aromatic. I would plant **Cinnamon Basil** if the walkway is used in the evening or after dusk. The heady scent of this Basil is almost sensual. These stately plants grow to 24" (60 cm).

- Upon entering a richly verdant tropical forest in Rarotonga, the Cook Islands . . . my guide stopped, picked a few stems of wild Basil and placed them behind his ear. Musing, I thought that this was the first step in some wonderfully natural spiritual ritual. I suppose it may have been, but the Basil was actually placed there to keep the bugs away.

- Basil's best friends in the garden are the Tomatoes. Always plant several Basil plants near your Tomato crop. Both plants benefit from each other in many ways. The Tomatoes seem to have an intensified flavour and the Basil grows larger than similar plants not planted near Tomatoes. After all, Basil and Tomatoes are the Italian version of kissing cousins, in pizza and pasta sauces.

- My pesto starts with freshly picked **Genovese Basil** as it tends not to have the overtones of mint that other selections do. Pine nuts are coarsely hand ground then milled with my finest extra virgin olive oil. Often, for an extra treat, I add about one-third fresh **Blue African Basil**, truly a special taste.

- The Basil varieties available on the market are divided into loose classifications. Sweet group, fancy sweet and other or exotics. Within these groups exist ruffled foliage varieties, purple leafed, tiny leafed and a host of others.

- Start Basil seeds indoors in cooler climates, usually in early April. Remember to afford the seedlings good bottom heat and plenty of fresh air. Apply a good fungicide at initial watering and repeat at transplant time.

Basil – Healer or Hoax?

- Snakebite, mosquito repellent and general insecticide are among the claims Basil have to a worldwide fame. Some suggest that Basil's name originates from *basilicus*, an ancient word for snake. Maybe there is something to its healing powers for venomous bites.

- Basil is regarded as a mild antiseptic and has an ability to calm the nerves.

- Historical references from the English herbalist, Nicholas Culpeper, "a scorpion was bred in a man's brain because he simply sniffed a Basil plant".

- Basil is used in Ghana by the Ewes to combat fevers, particularly malarial, as well as a general tonic for diarrhea, a gargle and a dressing for wounds.

Cleansing Herb

🌿 **Sorrel** has long been reputed as a cure and prevention for scurvy. For those of us who live far from Florida or California, the threat of such a disease may still linger, so growing a bit of Sorrel will provide some solace. Be careful, however, when Sorrel is considered for your salad bowl or soup pot. Listed as a plant with extremely high vitamin C content, this relative of Buckwheat is also somewhat laxative. Scurvy may no longer be your biggest concern!

🌿 Herbalists suggest that tea made from Sorrel is a wonderful appetite stimulant as well as a **diuretic and antiseptic**. So, in short, it will make you hungry, reduce your water and clean you out as it cleanses and kills any bugs . . . not bad for a spring tonic!

Easily Grown Herbs

🌿 **Camomile** is delightful as a carpet in an area that receives moderate traffic. Many British gardening books suggest this tough little herb as a lawn substitute. Perhaps great in Britain but in Central Canada it is best protected somewhat from too many feet. It does very well under a sitting bench or a willow chaise lounge in the garden. This way the plant still gets enough light to produce its little daisy-like flowers, yet is not trampled heavily.

🌿 **Hyssop** is a member of the mint family, easily recognized because of its square stems and leaves that are positioned oppositely on the stems. The flowers are arranged in whorls, giving the appearance of a tuft on the top of the plant. Colours range from red and white to bluish.

🌿 Hyssop is said to be a **great companion** for Cabbage plants. Actually this could look rather attractive. Many gardeners claim that the Hyssop keeps most of the destructive insects away from Cabbage and attracts beneficial insects such as bees to the garden. Perhaps the most delightful companion is **Grape**. Hyssop is said to enhance the flavour of Grapes as well as increase the yields.

- Annual and perennial flower beds are great venues for many herbs. In the backs of borders you may consider planting **Lovage** for its striking size and stately structure. I love to mix Lovage with liberal quantities of **Valerian** and **Anise Hyssop** in the sunniest borders I have.

- Deep in the rear of this border consider planting **Summer Savory** . . . a delightful herb. The rule book will allow you to poke a few Beans in with the Summer Savory, also, they are the best of garden companions. The azure blue/purple flowers of Summer Savory are complimented strongly by **Blue African Basil** and **Siam Queen Basil**.

Fondness For Fennel

- Most gardeners in Canada consider **Fennel** a foliage crop at best and discard the notion of ever having a bulb to sear on the barbecue. ***Nigella sativa*** is the name you would look for in botanical references, but it is also called ***Foeniculum vulgare***. Whatever you prefer to call it, this Dill-like plant is a kissing cousin to the Carrot.

- Start Fennel seeds very early in the spring, indoors, and baby them along until the end of May, or . . . buy the transplants early. A curious thing about Fennel is that it dislikes most vegetable garden plants, preferring to stand alone at the back of the border or cutting garden. Do not plant Fennel near Wormwood or Coriander. The latter will not make any seeds if it is within a few meters of Fennel.

- One of my favourite Fennel plants is rather dark in colour, offering a tremendous compliment to chartreuse-foliaged and flowering plants. The variety that is most common in garden centres is dubbed *F. vulgare* '**Rubrum**'. This is a variety of Bronze Fennel and, thankfully, is gaining popularity in Canada.

- A variety that is extra strong and withstands the odd gust of wind is '**Berfena**'. Speaking of wind, it is the seed of Fennel that, when made into a tea, is used to regulate the worst cases of flatulence. With this kind of information, I only wish that I was the person who got to name the varieties . . . I can think of a few dandies! *Foeniculum vulgare* '**Fartless Feather**' or perhaps *F. vulgare* '**Windless William**'.

- **Florence Fennel**, a popular variety in Italy (Finocchio in Italian) is *F. vulgare azoricum*. Unlike other sweet Fennels, this variety forms a large bulbous base, similar to celery in texture. This gorgeous base is popular in Italian cuisine for its crisp, **anise flavour**.

- The culture of these glorious feathers is rather simple. They like lots of sunlight and prefer very well-draining soil. The sweet Fennels, of the two, will tolerate poorer conditions. This makes sense as they are not being grown for their bulbs, simply to add colour and texture to the garden. I also have fairly good success on higher pH soils. They seem to produce fewer aphids and taller plants.

- The bulbs of the **Florence Fennel** are harvested just before there is a danger of frost. They will need all this time to size properly. If the soil is exposed to the hot sun, and not mulched, the volatile oils that give Fennel its **anise-like flavour** will be increased.

Dill Dilemma

- Unfortunately, poor old Dill has acquired the pseudonym of **"Dillweed"**. Perhaps this somewhat derogatory handle refers to the ease with which Dill is grown. Personally, I think that Dill is a marvelous plant, tall, graceful and wonderfully scented.

- Soil conditions for Dill are not dreadfully demanding. I am confident that Dill would grow in the cracks of the driveway. Safe to say that bumper crops of Dill will have had well-drained soil rich in compost or manures. Wind can play havoc with Dill plants in that they are tall, slender and blow over easily.

- The foliage of Dill is delicate and the favourite food of aphids. In order to deter these ravenous insects, I spray Dill with insecticidal soaps and allow it to dry on the plant. This is not a 100% foolproof method, but it does slow down the aphids. **Harvesting the foliage** is done in the early morning to obtain optimum freshness. The foliage is washed in cold water to remove the soap.

- **Dill seed** can be kept from year to year in a sealed glass jar or paper bag. The trick is to keep it in the dark, for some reason this affects the viability of the seed. Dill will also cooperate if it is planted in a **container**. I suggest that a Tomato cage be installed so that the plants have some support.

Thyme and Thyme Again

✦ Three distinct species of Thyme find their home in my gardens. **Woolly Thyme** (*Thymus pseudolanuginosus*), **Creeping Thyme** (*Thymus praecox*) and **Moonlight Thyme** (*Thymus nitidus* 'Moonlight'). Thymes are generally all mat-forming or fairly dwarf herbs with extremely aromatic foliage. A preference for strong sun may limit their use in the garden but strong drought tolerance makes them well worthwhile.

✦ *Thymus X citriodorus* '**Lemon Thyme**' is perhaps the most complex group of hybrids. Most of this group have lemon-scented foliage but there is much variance in shape, leaf colour and hardiness. The taller upright varieties are **excellent cooking herbs**. Like all Thymes, the soil should be well drained and somewhat on the lean or nutrient-starved side of the scales.

✦ Seed houses offer a vast selection of what I call **designer Thymes**. Varieties that have been selected or concocted to offer what I find to be mixed scent messages. **Coconut Thyme**, **Nutmeg Thyme**, **Lavender Thyme**, **Caraway Thyme** and **Oregano Thyme** are a few such offerings.

Bah . . . Humbug!

✦ *Marrubium vulgare* is commonly known as Horehound. The botanical name apparently comes from the Hebrew *marrob*, meaning bitter juice. The tag Horehound has evolved from the Celtic term for a fuzzy or downy plant, *har hune*. The magical attributes of this common herb are widespread. Ancient Egyptians regarded this plant as "seed of Horus" (the falcon-headed sky god) and honoured its ability to soothe sore throats.

✦ One recipe for **Humbug candy** calls for 4 oz. (115 g) fresh Horehound leaves, ½ teaspoon (2 mL) of crushed Anise seed and 3 crushed Cardamom seeds in 2½ cups (625 mL) of water. This mixture should simmer for about 20 minutes. Over a low heat add the strained liquid to 2 cups (500 mL) of white sugar and 1½ cups (375 mL) brown sugar. Boil until the sugar candies (soft-ball stage, 235°F/112°C) in a bowl of water. Pour the mixture onto an oiled tray and score it as if it were toffee. Store in waxed paper in a covered container.

Lavender Blue Dilly Dilly . . .

♣ Lavender has long been the herb associated with grandmothers. There are many varieties of this easily grown herb, but not are all as sweetly scented. Spike oil is derived from **Lavandula latifolia** and is most commonly used to perfume soaps. I suspect that the average nose couldn't tell the difference between spike oil and the **Lavandin** of the perfume trade. Easily grown, this sun-loving herb will produce coarse foliage, deep purple blossoms and an abundance of aromatic oil.

♣ The name Lavender apparently is derived from the latin **lavare**, to wash. This herb provided the favourite scent for bath waters and also for the laundry. Linens were rinsed in Lavender water to freshen them but also as a protection against insects. Today, a soak in a hot bath with Lavender oil as the aroma is purported to calm the nerves and relieve stress.

♣ The Lavender that we see in photographs growing in neat hedgerows in the south of France is actually a hybrid. The marriage took place some years ago in hopes of producing a plant which could produce abundant oils and yet be harvested mechanically with ease. The parents are **L. angustifolia** and **L. latifolia**. The new plants are often referred to as **Lavandin**, **Dutch Lavender**, **L. X intermedia**, or **L. hortensis**.

♣ One Lavender plant that is becoming increasing popular is **Spanish Lavender** or **Lavandula stoechas**. Although this plant is supposed to half hardy to 0°F (-17°C), I have not been able to overwinter it outdoors. My solution is to containerize this robust grower and bring it indoors for the winter. Recently, they appear on hoops, twisted and contorted to resemble burlesque topiary. These plants are much nicer grown as sturdy wee shrubs in the sunniest spot the garden has to offer.

♣ The most hardy of all the Lavenders is **Lavandula angustifolia 'Munstead'**. It tends to have a narrower leaf than most and grows as a fairly compact plant. Mine never get to be any higher than 24" (60 cm). These tough little gems produce copious amounts of bluish purple flowers which are well suited for drying. It seems that the heavier the snow cover the more of the specimen that survives. A cloche in the early spring will extend the season and protect from sudden early frosts.

Kissing Cousins

- **Marjoram and Oregano** are from the same genus of plant, it is only the species that is slightly different. If your garden is somewhat alkaline, these are wonderful herbs to grow. They both enjoy full sun, but a wise gardener will shade variegated or golden forms during the hottest part of the day.

- Thymol is an antiseptic oil that is found in **Oregano**. The same or at least a synthesized version of thymol appears in mouthwashes and oral antiseptics. I find that the flavour of Oregano is somewhat peppery and a bit green. The older leaves are what I prefer, as well as the small twigs. Placing sprigs of Oregano on the charcoal embers of the barbecue will infuse the smoke with a distinctively **Mediterranean scent**. The fresh leaves may contain higher concentrations of thymol and this may be what disagrees with my taste buds.

Sage Advice

- Sage has the reputation of being able to increase longevity, perhaps that is where the title "old sage" is born. Long living is a benefit when it comes to the perennial or herb garden. I have had sages of various shapes and sizes for many years. The best performer under the greatest amount of neglect is *Salvia officinalis*. It comes in such varieties as **'Tricolour'**, **purpurea 'variegata'** and **'Icterina'**. All the foregoing are multicoloured and have the same medicinal flavours as the species.

- Sages prefer to grow in **alkaline soils**, a benefit to the Prairie gardener. Although they can be grown from seed easily, I prefer to take softwood cuttings early in the season. With a small amount of rooting hormone, and moistened peat and Perlite® to root in, you will have new plants in about three weeks.

- *Salvia dorisiana* or the Fruit Salad Sage is a very curious plant indeed. I purchased a small plant about a year ago and proceeded to watch it stretch like a sunflower. A tender perennial with furry fragrant leaves, I suspected it would be fine as a houseplant. Amazingly, this tree has become the focal point of our master suite. I shred the leaves into **fruit salads** or use them as a decadent garnish with fresh fruit or tropical dinners, well worth the effort of keeping it constantly moist and shooing the whiteflies away.

- **Pineapple Sage** is a favourite pot herb in this household. It sports tiny crimson flowers and the most convincing aroma of pineapples imaginable. As with most of the Sages, this herb is edible and can be used fresh or dried. Personally, I prefer to use the leaves fresh, they tend to go a bit flat, in my opinion, once dried. Look for this diminutive darling under the name *Salvia elegans* or *S. rutilans*.

- *Salvia lyrata* **'Burgundy Bliss'** has just come to live in my garden. Although not a true herb, it is so closely related that I wanted to mention it. This selection was developed at the North Carolina Botanic Garden in the late 90s and kudos to the breeders. A delightful plant with dark, ruffled foliage in a tight rosette formation. It only grows about 12" (30 cm) high and should have white flowers with a blush of lavender for interest. I, for one, can't wait to see them.

- Diabetics might be interested in Spanish Sage or *Salvia lavandulifolia*. This Sage has leaves somewhat smaller than the garden variety and produces an oil that is harvested commercially. Apparently this is the only Sage that is ever used in Spanish cuisine; this may be my paella problem solved. Not only does it taste great, it is reported to **lower blood sugar levels** without affecting insulin levels.

Mediterranean Scents

- **Rosemary** is a grand and versatile plant. The particular cultivar that I have the best success with is one called **'Arp'**. The stems are quite sturdy and the amount of growth is remarkable; some seasons reaching over 12" (30 cm) in height. This herb is an ideal candidate as a little gift for the gardener who cooks.

- **Rosemary** is perhaps the most rewarding of all herbs to grow, both indoors and out. If you enjoy cooking, there is nothing that comes close to the flavours derived from fresh herbs. Rosemary and lamb or beef are classic. I grow *Rosmarinus officinalis* **'Arp'** with great success in a terra cotta container. Indoors for the winter it suffers from low light, often losing some inner foliage and stems. Once spring arrives it goes onto the deck and quickly recovers.

- *Rosmarinus officinalis* 'Tuscan Blue' is my newest addition to the herb garden. My intentions are to culture it as all the rest of the Rosemary selections, full sun, **alkaline soil** and dry between watering. The difference with this fine specimen is that the foliage has a bluish hue to it, a nice contrast to the greyish wood that eventually develops.

- Not all Rosemary are tall, sturdy, shrub-like herbs. A group of them such as the varieties '**Lockwood**' and '**Severn Sea**' are prostrate or trailing. I find that these plants tend to have smaller leaves and a rather prickly nature. I suspect that I am just spoiled with the large-leafed culinary varieties. One selection is called '**Pine**' **Rosemary** and has a definite scent of pine trees. This would not be ideal in cooking, but makes a novelty indoor tree.

- There is most likely not a single garden in Italy that doesn't have a patch of **Arugula**. I acquired some seed from the matron of my local Italian deli. Her seeds were lovingly collected from her over-abundant crop behind the store. Great plants and easily grown too, if you are looking for seed in the catalogues search for *Eruca vesicaria* or *E. sativa*. Arugula belongs to the Cabbage family, oddly enough, resembling Mustard in leaf form. The almost oily, bitter bite of Arugula is quintessential in spring Italian salata with good olive oil and balsamic vinegar.

- Arugula can be sown a couple of times in a season. I find that they prefer a cooler start to life, so **seeds sown in April** will germinate rapidly. The first few leaves should be left to size, then harvest them as they mature. If the season turns hot, forget the Arugula and sow again in August or early September for an autumnal harvest.

Migraine Headache Helper

- **Feverfew** is aptly named as it really does help reduce fevers and is particularly effective on migraine headaches. If you look at the "herbal remedies" available on the shelves in so many drugstores these days, the majority of headache relief potions contain feverfew or *Tanacetum parthenium*. At our house we grow both the species and the golden variety, *T.p. 'Aureum'*. Five or six fresh leaves ingested is the method preferred in our household, either in a salad or by themselves. They are not the tastiest garden treats, by a long stretch, but they do the trick.

- Once you have a Feverfew plant, there is little doubt that you will only ever have just one. They seed themselves to such an extent that I have dubbed them **the rabbits of the herb garden**. Their attractive Chrysanthemum-like foliage nestles close to the soil and perky daisy flowers erupt. The golden varieties look pleasant with the species but also work well mixed in with coarser-leafed plants such as Sorrel.

Ahh, The Herb That Relaxes

- **Valerian** is one of the largest herbs that I grow in my garden. One of the first to pop its head through the soil in the springtime, it ranges to nearly 6' (2 m) tall by summer's end. The flowers are umbels or clusters in a pale, pink-lilac and they smell divine. Often the literature neglects to mention the aroma but plays to the medicinal quality of this herb garden workhorse. Use them for structure and height in the rear of the bed and allow them lots of room. They are easily divided in the fall or early spring. The first signs of foliage are rather coppery coloured to burgundy, an attractive contrast with yellow tulips.

- Valerian attracts not only bees and butterflies to the herb garden, it seems to have an **intoxicating aroma for earthworms**. I for one, like to have a good population of earthworms in the garden, they usually mean a happy soil. Valerian also boosts the growth of nearby plants, apparently because it stimulates Phosphorus activity. Whatever the physics or magic, I grow it close to Roses, Carrots and Lovage . . . all of whom seem to be grand neighbours.

S O I L
dirt 'n' diggin'

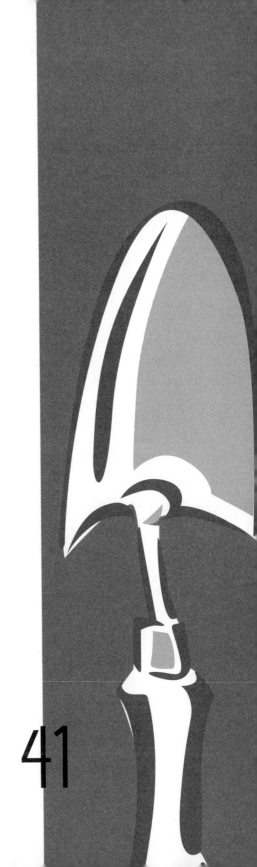

Dietary Supplements

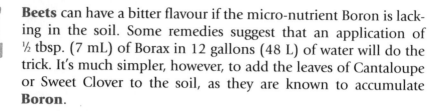

Beets can have a bitter flavour if the micro-nutrient Boron is lacking in the soil. Some remedies suggest that an application of ½ tbsp. (7 mL) of Borax in 12 gallons (48 L) of water will do the trick. It's much simpler, however, to add the leaves of Cantaloupe or Sweet Clover to the soil, as they are known to accumulate **Boron**.

Bone meal is a great supplement to add to almost any soil type, particularly at planting time. This product, as the name implies, is made from ground bones. It is used as a slow release provider of Phosphorus and also Calcium. Pet owners should be aware that some dogs may dig in an area where bone meal has been applied.

Heaps, Piles and Bins

Compost heaps, piles or bins start to thaw in late spring and will be ready to work shortly thereafter. If you have been adding kitchen vegetative scraps to your compost all winter, it is wise to **turn the mixture over**. Adding a thin layer of potting or garden soil on top will reduce the somewhat "woodsy" odour.

Compost heaps, piles and bins become inactive during colder weather. Once all the leaves are placed in the composter, water thoroughly and continue to add kitchen greens. The mixture will **freeze and thaw during the winter** which actually will speed up the decomposition process the following spring.

In very general terms, compost requires 25 to 30 times more high Carbon materials than high Nitrogen materials to work effectively. Some high Carbon materials are dry leaves, cornstalks, straw and paper. High **Nitrogen** materials are grass clippings, fruit waste and kitchen scraps. Higher ratios of **Carbon** base take longer to compost, whereas higher Nitrogen ratios have a foul odour.

Oxygen is an essential element to good composting. Adding small twigs will accommodate this requirement or a weekly turning with a fork is fine. Turning the pile too frequently will cool it down and thus slow or stop the process.

To provide a suitable environment for the active micro-organisms in the compost pile, the **moisture level** should be the consistency of a squeezed-out sponge. Too much water may make silage and anaerobic decomposition. Heat and Carbon dioxide are by-products of composting.

Composting can be accomplished without fancy equipment. Simply pile dry leaves, kitchen scraps and garden wastes in a sunny corner of the garden. Following the guidelines of more Carbon-based material than Nitrogen based, the heap will seethe and fume away until the compost is dark and soil-like. Infrequent turning of the heap will speed the process.

Knowing the **temperature of your compost heap**, pile or bin is not an essential factor in composting. Although there are many instruments sold for the convenience of avid composers, does it really matter?

Many people ask me if **pet feces** can be composted. My answer is, "sure", but don't use the compost around plants that you intend to eat. The potential does exist for canine or feline parasites and other nasties to transfer and survive composting.

When is the **compost ready to use**? Well, if you can put your hand into the heap, pile or bin and remove a handful . . . and not be able to distinguish Banana peels from coffee grounds . . . it's ready.

Compost heaps, piles or bins are not known to combust spontaneously. However, the possibility does conjure up a curious mental image, doesn't it?

Rhubarb leaves are often not placed into the compost. The suggestion that, as these leaves are poisonous, they will contaminate the compost is not exactly accurate. Composting reduces the materials to basic elements. Suit yourself, just don't eat the Rhubarb leaves.

Some cities have reported **reductions in landfill** by at least 5% because of composting programs. It makes sense to me, and look at all the great nutritional supplement you have for your garden for very little effort.

Compost tea is a wonderful botanical beverage, and easily made to boot. I use about a wheelbarrow full of finished compost in a 20-gallon (76 L) plastic garbage container. Simply dump in the compost, fill with water and stir the slurry daily for about a week. In warmer weather, less time is required to produce a grand tonic for container plants and special treasures.

Acid or Base?

Acidic soil is essential to the good culture of many plants. Peat Moss is the most commonly used soil amendment. Spring applications of **Sulphur will help acidify** and control many fungal infections. I have added well-composted steer manure and a good acidifier fertilizer to my plants that were growing in a very alkaline situation. This combination has worked well.

Rhododendrons, Azaleas and Bog Rosemary are three acid-loving plants. In the spring, it is wise to adjust the pH of the soil to ensure that it is "sour" enough. Liberal additions of Peat Moss, compost or well-rotted manure will acidify the soil slowly. Commercially prepared fertilizers are available to do the job, also.

Blueberries will enjoy an extra meal of fertilizer in July. These plants must have an acidic soil to produce good fruit. Apply a band of a balanced, granular fertilizer such as 10-10-10 about 4" (10 cm) from the base of the plants. **Do not use bone meal**.

Heather insists on an acidic soil. The easiest way to ensure that your garden soil is "sour" enough for these plants is to incorporate liberal amounts of Peat Moss. Acidifying fertilizers are available and should be applied in the spring and midsummer.

Clematis responds well to an **alkaline soil** condition. This gang of vining plants also prefer to have their roots in cool soil temperatures. Bone meal will encourage strong root development at the same time as adjusting the pH a few points upwards, causing the soil to become alkaline.

Diggin', Tillin', Torture

Rototilling or mechanically working a clay soil can be more detrimental than helpful. Nothing is more beneficial to a soil than a good **old-fashioned digging**. Clay soil particles are very small, the pounding of the tiller's tines breaks the clumps of soil into their finest state, like a powder. Once moistened, this powder turns to a "paste" and little or no air is present. Digging, on the other hand, allows larger clumps to be turned over, providing ample air space.

One of the punitive measures used when I was studying horticulture was to banish the transgressor to the vegetable garden to "double dig" the green manured areas. This did not mean that the offender had to dig the area twice, a much worse fate was bestowed. **Double digging** requires a trench to be dug at one end of the garden, two spades depths deep. The soil is taken in a wheelbarrow to the opposite end of the garden and piled. The trench is then filled with each successive row of soil, thus bringing the deepest soil to the surface. This process can be augmented by the addition of manure or other organic matter. Generally, the green manure crops, such as alfalfa, add sufficient nutrients to the soil.

Cultivating soil can be a somewhat relaxing chore. I use a three-pronged "cultivator" to scratch around the emerging plants and loosen up the soil. This action effectively dislodges any germinating weed seeds and allows the soil to dry somewhat. I enjoy cultivating as it allows me a time to check each of my plants, provides me with visible proof that I have accomplished something and it does keep the weeds in check.

Edging around the flower beds improves the look of the lawn and the beds. Using a sharpened **half-moon edger** is the easiest way to get this job done. Also, moist soil helps the job move along nicely. On clay or heavier soils, the angle of the cut can be almost vertical. Sandy, lighter soils, must be cut on a 45-degree angle or less. This function helps to keep the turf from creeping into the flower beds and, incidentally, increases the size of the planting beds rather quietly.

Square spades or English spades seem to be easier to use than the "spade-shaped" tools. I like to use a spade with a long handle and a sharpened edge. The "banjo" or round-mouthed shovel is a good all-purpose tool for good soil or for moving soil from a pile into the wheelbarrow. After you are finished with the tools, it is a good idea to apply a light coating of cooking oil to prevent rusting. Naturally, the tools are cleaned before the oil is applied.

Pottery or Pavement - Clay Soil Help

Classic amendments to a heavy clay soil are organic materials. Clay soils are often nutrient rich, but the soil particles so very small that there is little room between them for air or other materials. Organic matter introduces and houses a high percentage of soil organisms which are essential to a healthy soil. Adding manure, Peat Moss, leaf molds and compost can help loosen the clay soil but they must be added on an annual basis to really make a difference.

Flower pot syndrome is a term that I use for partial amendment of a clay soil. Let's say that a tree is to be planted and the soil is terribly heavy clay. What the gardener does most often is remove the clay soil to about two or three times the size of the root ball that is to be planted. In doing so, the sides and bottom of the prepared site are sheared with the spade, the clay actually becoming like a flower pot. The plant is installed in good amended soil and lots of water is added. **Drainage is compromised**, resulting in death by drowning.

Raised beds or planters are actually a good way to overcome lousy soil conditions. I have gardened for over 10 years on heavy soil, and finally have moved to raised beds for some of the more delicate and difficult plants. This way, I control the soil texture, fertility and tilth, the height of the planters and the drainage. If you are contemplating raised beds, I suggest that you make the beds as high as is comfortable for you to bend over. Taller gardeners may wish to have higher beds, shorter people, lower ones. As long as there is sufficient soil depth to grow your crops, the height is up to you. Timbers should be either cedar or pressure treated with the least toxic substance available. **Railway ties are treated with creosote, a toxin to plants.**

Sawdust and wood shavings are fine to add to a clay soil, provided they are hardwoods. I have seen a disastrous mess after an elated gardener added a considerable amount of pine and spruce sawdust to his garden. Mind you, there were no weeds, but the resins from the wood killed the crops, too. Shavings from Oak, Maple and Ash are great. They take at least three years to decompose, all the while adding structure to the clay soil.

Sand apparently was the recommended amendment for heavy clay soils. I am not supporting this notion at all, unless you are making concrete. Sand and clay, in particular the Prairie gumbo, make a solid marriage indeed, one that a spade can't penetrate. **Sand is better off in a box** for the kids to play in or under the swing set.

The Big Three N:P:K

N is for **Nitrogen** which is, to some, "the be-all and the end-all" of plant nutrients. Albeit, plants must have this element for growth, but enough is enough. This nutrient encourages strong and very rapid leaf growth. If you are a Lettuce farmer or own a golf course, Nitrogen is your friend. Otherwise, the growth that is encouraged is very soft and watery, particularly delectable to most insects and fungi. Reducing the amount of Nitrogen used on vegetable and flowering crops encourages strong, substantial growth.

P is for **Phosphorus**, the middle number in the fertilizer ratio. This is the nutrient that encourages strong root development and helps the flowers last. This nutrient is responsible for dark green foliage and very good roots and, also, it assists in development of good branches and stems.

K is for **Potash**, or **Potassium**, the final and perhaps most neglected nutrient in the fertilizer ratio. This nutrient is responsible for good stem and fruit development. Unfortunately, this nutrient is, more often than not, applied in very small amounts. This is the product that really helps small fruits, berries and many vegetable crops.

Deficiencies in any of the big three nutrients, **N, P, K** . . . will change the way your plants appear. A Nitrogen deficiency will have your plants looking insipid and rather yellowish. A Phosphorus deficiency will manifest itself in burgundy shades on the foliage and poor rooting. Potash, which is easily locked up in a soil, is necessary for strong stem growth. A deficiency appears by way of distorted leaves, poor rooting and very small stems. Often, the foliage appears burnt or browned.

pH is a term that you will frequently see in garden literature referring to the soil's acidity or alkalinity. Soils can be measured on a scale from 1 through 14 with 7.0 being neutral. Acidic soils are below 7 and alkaline soils are above. Prairie soils tend to be 8.0 or so whereas the Holland Marsh is below 6.5.

In One End, Out the Other – Manure

Farmyard manures are not the nicest commodity to discuss, unless you are a gardener or farmer. Older is better when it come to "gardener's gold". Weed seeds will live in the top few inches of a manure pile, and if you take your supply from here, there will be weeds in your garden for centuries to follow. Dig into the pile and get the oldest and the most protected portions for the garden. There is never enough of this stuff for the garden . . . believe me!

Green manure is the term given to a crop that is planted, after a cash crop has been harvested, with the intent of simply ploughing it under. Alfalfa is often used or relatives in the same family of Leguminosae. These plants have the ability to fix Nitrogen from the air into the soil. By ploughing the plants under after a season, you will add organic matter to the soil as well.

Composted manure is commonly available for the gardener's convenience where plants are sold. This product is weed free, a tremendous benefit when it comes to manures. I use a great deal each spring, from the vegetable garden, planters, window boxes to top-dressing the lawn. Once I was asked what the difference was between composted sheep and steer manure, the answer is fairly obvious to me, one comes from a steer, the other a sheep!

Application frequency of manure depends a great deal on the crop that you are growing. **Potatoes prefer no manure** or very little while Rhubarb, Lettuce and Cabbages would like a snack of it spring and fall. A clay soil will require liberal applications twice in the season for tilth and fertility. Most manures are beneficial for the structure they add to the soil rather than the fertility. 1:1:1 is the nutrient ration usually assigned to manures.

Canine and feline manures are not ideal candidates for the garden, particularly the vegetable garden. There is some chance that parasites may transfer through the vegetables to humans. However, there seems to be no reason not to use **pet manures** in the flower beds. Goodness knows, the cats from the neighbourhood are more than willing to accommodate.

Homemade Soil
– Artificial Intelligence

Perlite® is a substance that is added to most artificial soil mixes. It is the white, popcorn-like material which almost always floats when water is applied. In its raw state it is a clay-like material; when heated, it pops to form a particle that can hold up to 17 times its weight in water and still hold its form. This is of particular importance to the soil structure. **Perlite® is dusty** to work with and should be moistened while still in the bag. This process reduces the potential of injury from inhalation. Approximately one-third of a good general mix is Perlite®.

Vermiculite actually starts life as mica and was once used as an insulation for houses. This material is "spongy" and rather shiny in texture and appearance. Like Perlite®, it is used to add structure and water-holding ability to the soil. Unfortunately, Vermiculite breaks down after one season, rendering it a poor amendment for long-term mixes. Seeding mixes are comprised predominantly of fine Vermiculite. Sterile, inert and very inexpensive, this product will survive for some time yet.

Peat Moss is the cornerstone of artificial media mixes. Milled or shredded and prepared from Sphagnum Peat, this material is very old indeed. Actually, the Moss is not singularly Moss, there are shreds of twigs, bark and other botanicals in various stages of decay. The beauty of this product, as we find it, is that is relatively inert, weed free and will hold enormous amounts of water. The disadvantages include the fact that it doesn't last very long as a soil amendment and it acidifies the soil. I have often wondered where the three bales of Peat Moss that I added to the garden actually disappeared to!

Sphagnum Moss is rather unkempt, stringy Moss used a great deal in the floral industry. Actually, this Moss is more true to the way it is found in the bogs of Eastern Canada. I find Sphagnum Moss the ideal material to use in **wire hanging baskets**. It is matted enough to form a good barrier for the soil, yet a plant can be poked through without damaging the soil barrier. The City of Victoria, British Columbia, and other municipalities which still use traditional hanging baskets, must utilize enormous amounts of Sphagnum Moss.

The terms **sterile and inert** are commonly used to describe the manufactured components of a planting mix. Perlite® and vermiculite offer no nutritional benefit nor do they change the chemical composition of the mix, therefore they are "inert". Sterile should perhaps be changed to pasteurized, in some cases. Mixes are heated to 180°F (83°C) and cooked to kill most of the pathogens. This is actually pasteurization. Sterile could mean that the mix does not support any bacterial or microbial life, but I think that a mix needs to be steam treated or autoclaved to achieve that.

Triple Mix® is a common name given to a planting medium that is made up of 1 part topsoil, 1 part Peat Moss and 1 part Perlite®. In some regions this name refers to a type of garden soil that is 1 part topsoil, 1 part Peat Moss and 1 part manure.

Specialty mixes are on the markets for the convenience of the gardener. One good example is the hanging basket mixes. These mixes are particularly light, including Peat, Perlite®, vermiculite and a crystal-like material that holds water. This curious product swells once water is applied and forms a gelatinous glob in the mix. As the soil dries, moisture is obtained from these warehouses of water. I think that this is great stuff and should be added to window boxes, patio containers and even soil that tends to dry very quickly.

Specialty Soils and Mixes

Perhaps you have seen potted **orchids** with their straggly roots out over the side, and the pot full of bark chunks and foam. This is hardly a soil mix, but orchids must have extremely good drainage. The bark allows the roots to cling to something, yet the water is not absorbed. Large chunks of foam or Perlite® are used for the same reason. Shredded Tree Fern bark, Sphagnum Moss and finer bark chips are added to hold some moisture.

Orchids, for the most part, are **epiphytic plants**. This means that they live on a host plant, drawing nutrients from the air and not the host. The Bromeliade family has many epiphytic members. The large **Silver Vase Plant** or *Aechmea fasciata* is one of the most common. Although these plants are potted, the mix is very porous and is offering stability rather than nutritional value. The roots of epiphytic plants support and cling while the leaves absorb the moisture.

True Cacti require a specialized soil mix, not pure sand. Even in their home environment, Cacti enjoy some nutrient from the predominantly sandy soils. Light amounts of compost or organic matter are fine, as well as larger particles such as aquarium gravel or lava rock. **Cactus soil** must be well drained and offer little by way of Nitrogen.

Alpine soils are, to my mind, one of the most difficult to recreate. Scree or stone shards make up a good percentage of this type of soil with extremely well-draining material as the main base. Some **alpine soils** have compost or light leaf mold and sharp sand added for tilth.

Water plants such as Lilies require a heavy clay soil to support them. Generally, **Water Lilies** are planted in mesh containers and topped with pea gravel. A light soil will flush through the mess, leaving the Lily roots exposed. Finally a use for gumbo, it is great for Lilies. Manures and fine organic material are not used with water plants. They tend to either float or get so sodden that they do little good.

Dig with the left foot, edge with the right!

A spade is a spade to most people. There are so many different varieties of spades on the market that it is rather confusing. If in doubt, buy the one that feels right to you or looks like the one that Granddad had. **Trenching spades** have a long narrow blade, whereas **English spades** are blunt and rectangular. **Round-mouthed shovels** are the shape of a "spade" in the suit of cards, but rarely called a spade.

Shears and pruners are often interchanged for what should be quite separate chores. **Shears** look like large scissors and can be electric or manual. They are used to "shear"or trim hedges. I will not go on about trimming hedges and what a waste of valuable maintenance time this is . . . at least here! Pruning shears, pruners, or **secateurs** are hand tools that are used to prune or remove woody material. Perhaps the most versatile tool in the gardener's larder, these red-handled workhorses are not used to cut wire (at least not that I will admit to).

Loppers and pole pruners are tools that are used when the secateurs are just not strong enough, or you can't reach the limbs that you wish to prune. I prefer loppers which have wooden handles as I have bent too many metal ones. The anvil and blade of both tools should be **kept razor sharp** to facilitate the best cuts. The spring mechanism of the pole pruner should be oiled and adjusted from time to time to keep it operating at peak performance. Fibreglass, extendable poles are the best, in my opinion, for pole pruners. They are light, flexible and you don't get any slivers!

The lowly hoe is most likely the first tool that you will wear out. I received a hoe as a graduation gift; I wonder if there was a message in that? The hoe, and there are many different kinds, is generally a steel-bladed apparatus with a long wooden handle. Weeding is the major performance area for this tool. **Chop hoes** do just that, chop the weeds; **scuffle hoes** are slid along the soil to "scuffle" the weeds out. A **Dutch hoe**, at least this is the name my Dad gave it, is a thin rectangular blade, fastened to the open end of a "U", with a long handle. If you can find one of these, it can resolve many hours of back-breaking weeding, a wonderful piece of equipment to have.

Hoses, not the plural of hoe, are as varied as there are colours in the rainbow. I prefer one that won't kink. Mind you I have had vinyl, rubber and combinations of the same ad nauseam, and they still kinked! Of the entire gang of them, I still prefer to use the **100% rubber hose**, but the price is a bit scary. Sunlight is hard on hoses, so store them out of the bright light, and always away indoors for the winter months.

FUNGI

bugs,
pestilence
&
vermin

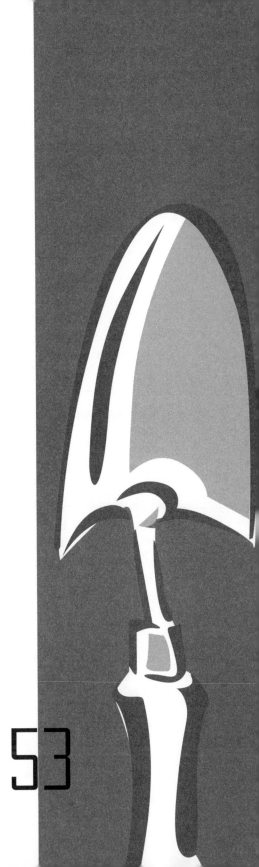

General Scourges

🦋 Tiny black flies, similar to fruit flies, may be circling your house-plants. These wee critters are called **fungus gnats**. Although they don't damage houseplants directly, they can be embarrassing. Treat the soil of all indoor plants with a drench of insecticidal soap or dust with the granular form of Diazinon™. Also, put a few drops of cooking oil in the sink traps, they lay their eggs in there.

🦋 **Mealy bugs** are perhaps the most difficult of all indoor pests to eradicate. These critters appear as cotton-like mats in the leaf axils and on the plant stems. The waxy cotton mass, which contains adults and eggs alike, repels most liquids. Rubbing alcohol dabbed on the white fluff is tedious but effective control.

🦋 **Delphinium** plants can be ravaged overnight by a nasty critter called a **Larkspur Worm**. It burrows down the central stalk of the plant and consequently destroys the bloom. Characteristically, this worm will roll itself inside new foliage. Dust the plants liber-ally with Rotenone® or comparable insecticidal dust. The trick is to apply as soon as you notice any damage.

🦋 *Cobaea scandens* is an annual vine, often described as a "sophis-ticated" climber, with fresh green leaves and absolute masses of indigo/violet flowers up to 1½" (4 cm) in diameter. Flowering until the first frosts of autumn, Cobaea can support several gener-ations of whitefly, spider mites and goodness knows what other critters.

🦋 The **Cabbage Butterfly** actually prefers to lay her eggs on or near **Nasturtiums**. These delightfully bright annuals are actually a ben-efit to the Cabbage growers. Plant a good number of Nasturtiums as far away as possible from Cabbage and related plants. The insect larvae will feed on the bait crop and the Cabbage will be spared.

A Fungus Among Us

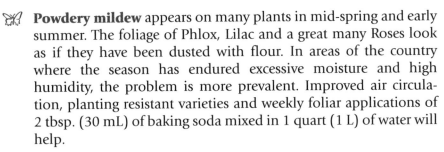

Powdery mildew appears on many plants in mid-spring and early summer. The foliage of Phlox, Lilac and a great many Roses look as if they have been dusted with flour. In areas of the country where the season has endured excessive moisture and high humidity, the problem is more prevalent. Improved air circulation, planting resistant varieties and weekly foliar applications of 2 tbsp. (30 mL) of baking soda mixed in 1 quart (1 L) of water will help.

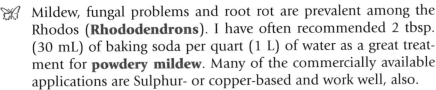

Mildew, fungal problems and root rot are prevalent among the Rhodos (**Rhododendrons**). I have often recommended 2 tbsp. (30 mL) of baking soda per quart (1 L) of water as a great treatment for **powdery mildew**. Many of the commercially available applications are Sulphur- or copper-based and work well, also.

Black knot is a disease that attacks **Cherry**, **Pear**, **Chokecherry** and many related trees. This disease is characterized as a black, irregular and swollen amount of tissue attached to the branches. Removal is essential, as is hygiene. Clean your pruning tools, after each cut, with gas line antifreeze or isopropyl alcohol. This will prevent the spread of this highly contagious disease. Discard the affected branch immediately.

Rose growers are more than familiar with the range of fungal infections that come with the territory. For many years, gardeners applied copper- or Sulphur-based products and, more recently, broad-spectrum fungicides. Unfortunately, this exuberance for broad-spectrum products may have backfired as many strains of **fungi are now resistant**. If you must use a fungicide on **Roses**, I suggest that Sulphur is still the safest of all to use. It has been applied since the 1800s with little adverse reaction.

Gooseberries and Currants suffer dreadfully from powdery mildew and a host of other fungal conditions. The leaves appear to have been dusted with a white powder, especially if the weather has been warm and the nights damp. Two tbsp. (30 mL) of baking soda mixed in 1 quart (1 L) of water makes a fine spray to combat this problem.

- Roses which are sprayed with an **anti-transpirant** often do not suffer from as many fungal-related problems. These products are sold under a variety of names, but generally are all water soluble and break down over time on the Roses. The notion is that the pores on the leaves are coated with this "paraffin-like" substance, reducing the amount of moisture loss. At the same time, fungal spores have a difficult time establishing on this slick surface.

Winged Vampires

- Mosquitoes can ruin a day of gardening. Clean out your eaves troughs, a small amount of standing water is enough for mosquitoes to breed in. Standing pools of water, persistent puddles and containers that hold any moisture should be drained. Keep a lid on your rain barrel and over turn any garden containers that may hold water.

- It is only the female 'skitters that bite! The guys don't have the correct equipment. Apparently blood is crucial to the development of the eggs.

- Mosquitoes can survive for many years, in a dormant stage, until the climatic conditions are right.

- There are at least **seven species of mosquito** in Canada, all of which seem to be oversized.

- How big is that singular mosquito in your tent or bedroom in the middle of the night? I think they are a special classification, bred for attacks under stealth and below radar.

- Do the **largest mosquitoes** hail from Manitoba, Saskatchewan, Alberta, Ontario or Newfoundland?

- Spraying a chemical compound to kill mosquitoes is really a waste of time. These insects have a keen sense of smell and are agile, to say the least. Combine this with the fact that the chemical droplets must come in contact with the bug to kill it. Usually, mosquitoes smell the product, head for the hills until things calm down, then return. Citronella scent is an effective deterrent.

- **'Skitters can float on the wind** for huge distances. If your home is anywhere near a body of water or untreated zone, look out . . . the paratroopers and reconnaissance troops will arrive in droves.

🦋 The most effective treatment for mosquitoes is **preventative measures**. Standing bodies of water like ponds, sloughs, puddles and wetlands should be treated with a **non-toxic larvicide**. These products provide a film over the water surface that affects the respiration of the mosquito larvae. The only caveat here is that everyone must participate in the project, otherwise the untreated water becomes home to zillions of insects. Many municipalities are finally seeing the wisdom of this style of management.

🦋 One of the **biggest hoaxes**, in my opinion, is the **"Mosquito plant"**. Touted as some genetic mutant between Citronella and Geranium, this "Wizard of Oz" is billed as having the ability to eliminate mosquitoes. Have you ever grown one? That's ok, they are nice-looking plants and they do have a Citronella-like smell. However, Basil is a much better insect-repellent plant.

Trapeze Artists

🦋 Prairie gardeners are more than familiar with **Cankerworms**. These distasteful worms dangle from tree branches by a silky thread. April is the time of the year sticky bands should be applied to Elm, Apple, Maple and Chokecherry trees. Place the band at about shoulder height to avoid getting caught in the trap yourself.

🦋 The Spring Cankerworms emerge from the base of the tree where they have overwintered as adults. The pregnant females parade, like the lemmings of the insect world, through the bark furrows to the budding leaves in the canopy. The eggs are laid and within a few short weeks, about the same time as the fresh foliage appears, the ravenous young emerge.

🦋 **Fall Cankerworms** march up the trunks of Elm, Maple and most fruit trees in September. Apply a sticky band to these susceptible trees, approximately at chest height. I use a combination of fibreglass insulation, polyethylene, duct tape and white axle grease. This not-toxic trap should be removed when the snow flies.

- Leaf Rollers, Cankerworms, Cabbage Worms, Loopers and other Caterpillars are a menace in May. Products containing a bacterium called **Bt** are formulated to destroy this family of insects without harming beneficial insects, birds or animals. Trade names that are available are **Dipel®** and **BTK®**.

- I have found that the most effective sticky agent is white axle grease. This material can withstand very cold weather and still retain its adhesive qualities.

- Some people grind Cankerworms into a slurry, add water and spray the mixture directly on infected trees. Perhaps the smell of dead Cankerworms is a deterrent for the munching masses.

- **A typical Cankerworm infestation** can strip a fully grown Elm tree of all its foliage. Generally, if the tree is in reasonable health, it will regrow **a second flush of leaves**. Most trees have a reserve of energy large enough to produce about one-third of the foliar density.

- In many Prairie cities, the Cankerworm infestations are so bad that sidewalks under trees become dangerous to walk on. Insect droppings and the Cankerworms themselves actually make the concrete slippery.

- A spray of **insecticidal soap** is an effective control for Cankerworms. These sprays do not kill the insects on contact, they must ingest it. However, they stop feeding immediately (this is a good thing) and die of dysentery within 72 hours.

Munching Critters

- Squirrels can often destroy even the most protected lily garden. Try covering the bulb beds with chicken wire to prevent them from digging into the soil. **The only bulbs that squirrels seem not to relish are Fritillaria**.

- Squirrels are a garden pest that are not only cunning but some-what difficult to discourage. One gardener suggested to me that attaching Rose prunings, to the trellises and wires used by the squirrels as runways, will slow them down considerably. This may be a bit tedious to construct but apparently it is effective.

Tanglefoot® is an extremely sticky substance used in the garden for a number of pests. One such pest is the squirrel. A viewer relayed to me how he had coated all his bird feeders with this product to **discourage the squirrels**. I am not confident that the squirrels kept away, I suspect they cleaned their feet and found an alternative route to the garden.

According to some people, there are a few plants that are "**deer-resistant**". I have not had much success in this department, but then again, my garden is not on the outskirts of the city or near a large greenspace. Aquilegia or Columbine is easily grown, however, it normally succumbs to the Larkspur Worm before the deer can get it. Baptisia or False Indigo may taste bad to deer, and Digitalis is avoided by most animals.

Moles can cause enormous damage in a garden. These subterranean rodents munch roots and entire plants, leaving mounds in sod and in the garden. One plant that will discourage an invasion is *Euphorbia lathyris* or **Caper Spurge**. As with many of its relatives, this Spurge has milky latex sap that can cause dermatitis. This may be the exact substance that drives the moles away. If you plan to use this plant, be advised to wear gloves while handling it. Instruct children not to touch this plant, or provide a barrier around it.

Cats can make a real mess of and in your garden. I am fond of cats and wish to discourage them from my garden in the most humane way that I can. The easiest discouragement is to lay Rose and Raspberry trimmings around the area that the cats frequent. The thorns suggest that kitty "go" elsewhere.

The perennial plant *Ruta graveolens* or Rue is said to be a deterrent to cats. I have planted several of these interesting herbs in my garden. It took me several years to realize that it was not the plant itself that kept the felines at bay, but the clippings. So, when the plants reach about knee high, cut them back and lay the branches in the areas frequented by "puss". The odour is rather "oily" to my nose, but **very unattractive to cats**

'Wig Solutions

Earwigs are some of the most disgusting of all garden critters. Their abdominal pinchers are not used on humans, but they look as if they could be. **Earwigs are found where Dahlias grow**, and they are nocturnal. Some controls suggest traps of cooking oil and soy sauce, but the most effective, to date, is a plant. **Cuban Oregano**, a type of Plectranthus, apparently discourages these pests entirely.

Physical traps for Earwigs can be as simple as a rolled-up newspaper, strategically placed in the garden at dusk. The following morning the paper will be home to many Earwigs, which can be disposed of easily.

Garden Gnomes

Onion Maggots tend to obliterate an entire row, one plant at a time. In fact, these "subterranean chainsaws" move in straight lines as they feed. One solution is to plant the Onions in random clumps, to avoid the military-like eradication of your Onion crop.

Apple trees, Plums, Apricot and **Crabapples** are all somewhat susceptible to **fungal blights and rusts**. There are a host of "new" products on the market that purport to be the best yet but, to my mind, the older controls are still pretty good. The regime that is most effective for Apples is to spray the tree with dormant oil and lime Sulphur in April, before the leaves show. Once the leaves are out and the blossoms spent, you can apply the copper-based Bordeaux mixture. Sulphur is often applied once Apples start to form. Remember, humid or damp summers bring on the worst infestations of fungus and rust.

Weeds not only rob nutrients from the cultivated garden plants, they often harbor insect pests. A wise gardener will deal with weeds, as soon as they germinate, with a sharp hoe. At this tender stage they are easily removed, and have not had time to deplete the soil's goodness.

Flea Beetles are very common pests in Prairie gardens. The main reason that there are such huge infestations is due to the Canola crop. **Flea Beetles love Canola**, but when populations are large, they move to the veggie patch and the flower garden. Chemical sprays are less than effective on these hungry vermin, but soapy solutions will slow them down. Insecticidal soaps or even a surfactant causes them to fall ill with serious dysentery. Eventually, they die. **Avoid yellow flowers in your garden**, these tempt the Beetles to visit.

Pear slugs appear as black, tear-drop-shaped insects on a variety of plants in late June. Most commonly, they are found on Cotoneaster hedges, in some regions of Canada. These insects seem immune to popular garden insecticides. A solution made from 4 quarts (4 L) of water, 5 Rhubarb leaves, 2 tbsp. (30 mL) of chili peppers and ¼ cup (60 mL) of pure soap works very effectively.

Cabbage Butterflies will doubtless be invading the vegetable garden. Rather than waiting until they appear and applying a chemical product, simply plant Nasturtiums at the opposite end of the garden. The **Cabbage Butterfly prefers to eat Nasturtiums** over Cabbage. This "trap" works even in the smallest garden.

Cabbage Butterfly larvae can decimate a crop in very little time. Planting good-sized plants will deter the worms, but if you have these insects try dusting the Cabbage heads with Rye flour or sprinkle them with salt while there is still dew on them. Some people apply sour milk into each Cabbage to encourage the worms to leave.

Wormy Apples and insect-damaged Plums can dishearten any gardener. In early July, rake up all the windfalls and either bury them or send them to the landfill. This fruit will contain the larvae and eventually the pupae of the insect which lays the eggs in the first place. Do not compost them!

Blossom-end rot on Tomatoes is one of the most disheartening conditions of the season. This blight occurs at the bottom end or blossom end of the Tomato, manifesting itself as a black or brown watering mark. The spot continues to decompose, rendering the fruit useless in most cases. Most garden literature will suggest that this is caused by a Calcium deficiency in the soil. Perhaps, but I always suggest that good air circulation be established by planting the plants further apart. Also, **never water the foliage at night**. Add some Calcium, if you wish, in the form of oyster shell and see what happens.

Cutworms are the sawyers of the vegetable patch. These wiry wee worms must have teeth of tungsten or some such metal. They chew their way through just about anything in the garden, and leave it there to rot. One of the best defenses against these critters is to plant susceptible plants, like Tomatoes, in **tin can collars**. Some people use waxed milk cartons for the same purpose. Simply cut the ends out of a large food tin and slide it over the Tomato transplant. Ensure that it is pushed into the soil to a depth of 3 to 4" (8-10 cm), at least. The deeper the better! This collar will also act as a water reservoir for the plant.

Slimers

Slugs are, at best, ugly critters. There are as many treatments to eradicate them as there are gardeners, I am sure. Generally they prefer moist, woodland conditions, but they are infesting even the more arid regions of the Prairies. The overpopulation of these molluscs may be in part due to the importing of nursery stock from damper climes. Eggs and adults hitch a ride in the nursery containers, and emerge as immigrants in your garden.

Knowing where slugs lay their eggs and set up housekeeping helps when it comes time to apply your control. I have found that border areas, such as the zones between timbers and concrete or soil, harbor millions of slugs. The areas where sod meets soil or timbers are additional haunts. Applications of **boiling water** in these areas reduce the numbers significantly and are, of course, non toxic.

Slug baits generally contain a chemical called Metaldehyde®. This product has some affect on slugs but, for the most part, I feel that it should not be used. The slugs that actually succumb to this toxin can cause more harm to the beneficial wildlife of your garden. If a bird should ingest a slug poisoned with Metaldehyde®, it too can die. This **secondary poisoning can also affect pets**.

One rather peculiar yet effective control for slugs is to place **Grapefruit rinds** in the garden. The half shells will actually house a number of slugs and the citric acid apparently does them no good. In the morning, simply pick up the slug condos and dispose of them. I would not compost them.

Control Programs OR the S.W.A.T. Team

Rhubarb makes an excellent insecticide for soft-bodied insects such as aphids. Chop about six large **Rhubarb leaves** and place them into a 2-gallon (8 L) bucket of hot water. Stir the mixture and allow it to sit at least overnight. Strain the mixture, compost the leaves and spray the resulting tea on your aphids. The active ingredient is oxalic acid. A little insecticidal soap added to the tea increases adhesion to the plants, and to the aphids, too.

Rotenone® is a dust that is made from the roots of the Derris plant. **Just because a product is derived from a botanical base does not mean that it is not toxic.** As a matter of fact, many botanical insecticides are more potent than their synthetic cousins. Derris was discovered in the jungles, where native people used the root to stun fish. This method is sure a lot easier than line and hook or net. However, while Derris root only stuns the adult fish, it kills the babies. In the long run, if this practice is overused, there would be no fish to stun. Don't apply Rotenone® near the fish pond!

Dormant Oil is a light oil similar to mineral oil. As the name implies, it is used when plants are dormant or not growing. This product is a broad-spectrum insect control, particularly for species which overwinter in egg or larval stages. The oil is applied in the late spring, when the plants and insects are just awakening from winter. The oil simply coats the insects or eggs and they asphyxiate.

Yellow is the favourite colour of whiteflies. This information helps when you wish to trap them in the greenhouse or at home. Install sticky yellow, plastic tags to plants that are susceptible to whiteflies. If you can't find the tags already made up, use a sticking agent such as petroleum jelly or white axle grease and apply it to strips made from recycled food containers. Every few days, clean the tags with a tissue, re-stick them and place them back near the plants. Sounds simple but it is really effective.

Thrips are ravenous, slender bugs that tend to show up on African Violets, Gladiolus and many blue flowers. It stands to reason that, if they are so fond of blue, we might be able to trap them using this colour. Use the same technology as for whitefly traps, this too works like a charm. Remember though, thrips are harder to catch, have longer life spans than whitefly and they seem to be born pregnant.

 **Mealy bugs** rank quite high on the disgusting scale for household bugs. Not only do they produce a cottony mass, under which their eggs are laid, they have a waxy outer coat. This coat repels all liquids, so spraying them with anything is useless. The only product that is somewhat effective is **isopropyl alcohol** dabbed on the cottony masses. The alcohol gets through the waxy coating and kills adults and eggs. It is safe to say that once you see cotton, the infestation needs to be dealt with immediately. Just because you have cleaned the entire plant once, don't assume the job is over. Check in about 14 days to see if there are signs of bug life.

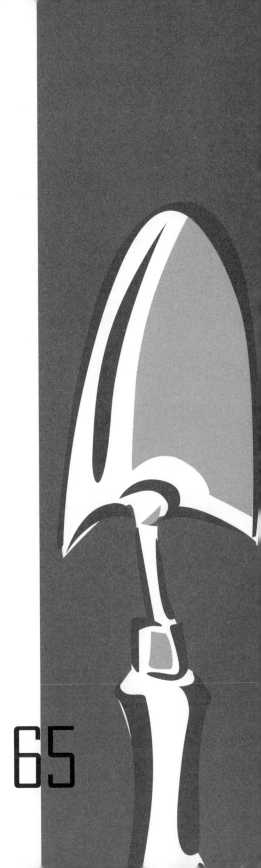

VEGGIES

fruit

&

other

edibles

65

Tom Tomato

Tomatoes require a head start of about six to eight weeks before they are to be transplanted into the garden. I am asked so many times "when" to do whatever it is for the best success. As you may know by now, there really is no "best time" for gardening but, rather, tried and tested times.

Tomatoes that have been sown before the first week of April are generally well on their way to becoming leggy and stretched before planting time in late May. Pre-germination of Tomato seed is not entirely a bad idea to ensure viability.

I like to **warm the soil prior to planting the Tomatoes**. Stretch a sheet of black or clear, heavy-mil poly over the planting area at least two weeks prior to planting. The sun will warm the soil under the plastic remarkably, often speeding up the harvest by two weeks, at least. I recommend leaving a **mulch** of some sort around Tomatoes. Be it grass clippings (brown), black plastic or compost. The mulch helps prevent pathogens from splashing up on the lower leaves of the Tomatoes, maintains a consistent moisture level, warms the soil and discourages weed growth. Warm soil during the night for Tomatoes will increase the yields incredibly.

If you think that you may have the largest Tomato ever grown, the benchmark that must be exceeded is 7 lbs., 12 oz. (3.5 kg), in 1987. Remember that Tomatoes love a good dose of salts, too. Two tbsp. (30 mL) of **Epsom salts** in 1 quart (1 L) of water is a great tonic. Apply this mixture weekly and see if you can beat the champ.

A couple of degrees of warmth makes all the difference in the world to the fruit set of a Tomato. If you mulch the plants with brick chips, stone or something that will absorb daytime heating, it makes the job easy. The stone releases heat during the cooler evenings, increasing the ambient temperature close to the Tomato by a few degrees. Also, the **extra heat helps deter fungal infections**.

Tomato seeds should be sown about two months prior to the last frost day in your zone. For those of you who start seed earlier, ending up with "Jack's Beanstalk Tomatoes", here's a solution. The stems of leggy Tomatoes can be laid into the planting site, allowing only the top portion of the plant to be above the soil line. The stem will grow roots and eventually produce a sturdy plant.

Tater Tips – Potatoes

🍅 French fries, poutine, scalloped or baked, these tubers are perhaps the most popular of all vegetable in North America. Originating in Peru, the simple Potato comes in hundreds of shapes and sizes and, yes, even colours. I have grown a variety called **'All Blue'** and, indeed, as the name implies, the tubers are dark blue. When the flesh is cooked, the royal blue turns to a sky blue, not a real hit with the kids. I thought it was good marketing when I suggested **"Blue Chips"** be served when our investment broker came to dinner.

🍅 Potatoes are somewhat prone to a disease called **Potato scab**. This ugly disfigurement of the tuber can be controlled without harmful chemicals being added. Potatoes can tolerate a higher pH without forming the scab if the soil is well balanced and nutrient rich. Prairie soils tend to be very alkaline (a high pH about 7.5) and scab is quite common there. Treat this type of soil with small amounts of compost or Peat Moss, but avoid manures. Higher organic content in the soil tends to bring the soil pH to the desired range, about 5.0 to 6.5.

🍅 **"Taters"** are planted from seed Potatoes or segments of seed Potatoes. Using old, leftover Potatoes from the supermarket is not the best idea. Often, a variety of diseases accompany these Potatoes, and some are even treated with chemicals or radiation to prevent them from sprouting in the store. Serious Potato growers will use **certified seed Potatoes**. These tubers are often smaller than the bakers you find in the store. They will have several "eyes" or buds. If the seed Potato has lots of eyes, cut the tubers so they have **two eyes minimum**.

🍅 In most of temperate North America, Potatoes are planted in the early spring, around the same time as the early bulbs are in bloom. I prefer to prepare the soil with a spade, digging a full spade's depth and turning the soil over. To prepare the seed Potatoes, cut them to have a couple of eyes at least, then allow them to dry overnight in a paper bag in a cool, dark location. **Dust the chunks with agricultural Sulphur** to help prevent any fungal infections. Sulphur is also a good way to lower the pH, or acidify an alkaline soil.

I have grown Potatoes and not hilled them at all . . . blasphemous some might say, but the method worked well. The Potato patch was growing nicely and it looked like the time to hill. This is usually done when the stalks are setting flower. My holiday period was just around the corner, and I was going to be away from my garden for a lengthy period of time. No time to hill once, let alone the preferred twice. I loaded the plants with a thick layer of dried grass clippings to a depth of 6" (15 cm). This mulching method was viewed as curious by the rest of the gardeners in the public garden. In spite of their skepticism, my Potatoes produced a grand crop under the mulch, and were they ever clean. I hardly had to wash them as they had formed close to the soil surface, under the clean mulch.

"A-maize-ing" Corn

Maize, as Corn was known to the Aztecs and indigenous North Americans, has been a staple for centuries. **Corn is the heaviest feeder in all the garden**, with a special appetite for Nitrogen. Knowing this, you may decide to grow the Corn in an area removed from the bulk of the vegetable garden. These plants do not have a very deep root system, so fertilizers and organic soil amendments need to be applied near the surface. Compost, manures and blood meal all work well on the Corn plant. Partners to plant with Corn are the legume family. Peas and Beans have the ability to fix Nitrogen from the air into the soil. Corn loves this arrangement, as do many gardeners.

Water is crucial to the success of Corn. Some gardeners will plant three or four seeds in a depression, so that the water will be captured and settle around the plants. It is a good idea to increase the amount of organic content in the soil that will be used for Corn. Organic material will help the soil retain more moisture. Some gardeners have mulched their Corn crop to ensure that soil temperatures do not fluctuate excessively, another important aspect to Corn culture.

🍅 Corn has its highest sugar content in the early morning. If you are a connoisseur of Corn, you'll know to **pick the evening's meal first thing, before the sun has warmed the husks,** and store them in the refrigerator until dinnertime that evening. I would avoid buying Corn on the cob from roadside vendors, if possible. Who knows how long those cobs have been sitting in the sun? Speaking of sweetness, the many varieties on the market touted as "Supersweet whatever" should be planted in separate blocks in the garden to avoid cross-pollination. Sowing the seeds about two weeks apart will also prevent this problem.

🍅 **Pumpkins** are a traditional companion crop with Corn. I suspect that the hairy stems and leaves of the Pumpkins, and the abundance of foliage, are more than likely a deterrent to raccoons. I am not sure what will work to keep raccoons from eating the Corn, it is one of their favourites. Some gardeners go to great expense to install electric fence wire low to the ground around the Corn, while others manipulate scarecrows and radios blaring rock and roll music. Whatever your preferred methods of discouraging varmints in the Corn patch, remember that the **raccoons are clever** and you must be at least one day ahead of them to get the Corn first.

🍅 As a child, I was taught to plant Corn seeds to the tune of a nursery rhyme. One for the cutworm, two for the crow, three for raccoons and the fourth to grow. Albeit, it may have helped me get the chore finished for my parents, **there really is some benefit to planting Corn in groups**. The plants need each other for support and they depend on one another to cross-pollinate. Corn is grown in blocks of shorter rows rather than one or two long continuous rows. The blocks are easier to pollinate. The soil is best warmed prior to planting, either by covering the area with black plastic or a good heavy mulch. In northern climates, **Corn is sometimes planted as a transplant** to ensure a harvest before frost.

Of Cabbages and Kings

Cabbage is a very popular garden crop and not that difficult to maintain. Other members of the Cabbage family include Brussels Sprouts, Broccoli, Cauliflower and Mustard. Classification for Cabbages is broken into four groups; early sweet green, late-season sweet green, red and savoy. The latter is the variety that appears to have seersucker leaves. Sun lovers, these plants **require about 12 weeks of good weather** before frost for a fall crop. In the warmer regions of North America, Cabbages will tolerate light shade in the afternoon. They love water until they are forming their heads, then slow down a bit so as not to cause splitting. Although not that fussy about who they are planted beside, Cabbages do not get along with Tomatoes, Strawberries or Pole Beans.

I have never grown Cabbage from seed sown directly into the garden. Alas, I have always gardened in colder regions of the country and relied on transplants. **Cabbage can take cooler weather** but, to be careful, the young transplants should be covered with a cloche or other frost-inhibiting device in the very early spring. I like to **grow them near the Carrots, Onions and Beets**, if I plant any. They seem to enjoy a higher pH or alkaline soil, so if you are a Prairie gardener, Cabbage should do well for you. They are heavy feeders and awfully fond of Potassium. The addition of wood ashes was used by early settlers to help boost the supply of Potash.

The roots of the Cabbage family are all very close to the surface. This can be a bad thing, especially for untrained weeders. The sharp edge of the hoe will chop off a Cabbage just as quickly as a thistle. Mulching will eliminate many of the weeds and the need to constantly be tilling the soil. The **mulch also maintains a more constant soil temperature**, thus reducing the splitting that often occurs on Cabbage.

One way to increase your yield of Cabbage is to encourage each plant to **produce more than one head**. Now, this may seem like science fiction to most, but try this trick and see what happens for you. Cut off the head of your early Cabbage, leaving a stump. Using a very sharp knife, make an incision across the full width of the stem, about ¼" (1 cm) deep. Continue to feed and water the Cabbage plants as you did previously. In a matter of a few weeks, there will be several tiny Cabbage heads forming. Allow this secondary crop to size as large as possible before the killing frosts. **They may get as large as baseballs**.

🍅 **Cabbage Butterflies** are a real nuisance to the home gardener and devastating, I assume, to a commercial grower. There are many chemical treatments and some non-toxic approaches that are relatively effective controls. If you choose to use a chemical product, ensure that it is registered for use on vegetables or edible crops and apply it strictly according to label directions. Non-toxic sprays, such as those made with a bacillus, work more slowly. One must see the larvae of the Butterfly and then spray. One excellent method of control is a **bait crop of Nasturtiums**. The Cabbage Butterfly lays her eggs on these plants as the young larvae prefer them to Cabbage. Maybe we should rename the Cabbage Butterfly "Nasturtium Moths"! To decoy the butterflies plant Nasturtiums as far away from your Cabbage as possible.

Sorrel and Other Spring Greens

🍅 Sorrel, not the most common garden green in North America, is big in Europe. I have a few plants in my potager and enjoy an early spring snack. *Rumex acetosa* is the botanical name given to Sorrel, well named as the taste is quite "acetosa" or like vinegar. The reason the taste is bitter is due to the high content of **oxalic acid**, the same material that makes Rhubarb leaves poisonous. So do not eat too much Sorrel. Further to the oxalic acid, Sorrel will clean you out quicker than you can say oops! This I know from experience and a grand recipe for Sorrel soup. The neighbours will no longer accept my culinary masterpieces.

🍅 Two kinds of Sorrel are common. The smaller-leafed variety is called French Sorrel (*Rumex scutatus*) and tends to have less of a "bite" than its larger-leafed cousin, Garden Sorrel (*Rumex acetosa*). I grow the garden variety in semi-shade, at least this is so for the summer. During the spring season, the lack of leaves on the trees affords more sun into the potager. Covering the emerging plants with a Kozy Kote® or cloche, speeds up the growth of leaves. They are not useable in the summer months, or as the leaves mature, as they are too bitter and dangerously high in oxalic acid. I use a rich soil with oodles of composted manure added annually. They enjoy water and get along well with the huge Lovage plant that lives beside them. In some of my readings I have come to discover that one non-culinary use of Sorrel was to bleach linens of ink, rust and mold stains. **No wonder it cleans out the digestive system so well!**

- **Dandelion greens** are actually not bad in a salad, the trick is to harvest them early in the day and when they are very young. In France they grow Dandelions in beds and some North American pioneers fenced off their Dandelion beds to keep out the deer. These leaves actually have some medicinal qualities attached to them, in particular for bladder problems. Most early greens are high in vitamins and some minerals also. It is only common sense to use leaves that have not been subjected to any pesticides. Rarely is there a shortage of this easy salad green.

- **Chive flowers** are very decorative and often the first flower open in my garden. I used to place Chives as merely a garnish on spring salad plates, but now I include the flowers in the salad. Tear the blossoms apart and sprinkle them into a green salad for an Onion overtone. Chives are good at deterring Apple scab and mildew, as well they help to keep aphids out of the garden.

- If colour and texture are important for your spring salad table, try adding the almost neon-coloured flowers of perennial Geraniums to the bowl. *Geranium pratense* or **Cranesbill Geranium**, in all of its cultivated forms, looks tremendous with greens. The taste is rather tart and has medicinal hints on my tongue. These flowers are available for most of the spring and right through the summer season. The leaves of Geraniums can be **used to flavour jellies**, Crabapple specifically, as well as sponge cakes and other light baking. Place a clean leaf in the bottom of the pan and bake it in, or set a small leaf in the jelly jar.

Lettuce – Lactuca – l'amore

🍅 Aphrodite is said to have laid the dead Adonis on a bed of Lettuce leaves with hopes that the healing properties of this now salad herb would revive him. I am not sure of the outcome, but it is safe to say that Lettuce has been around a long time indeed. The classification of this leafy producer is roughly according to shape and size. **Leaf Lettuce** ranges from ruffled to red to bi-coloured leaves which produce loose rosettes in about a month from sowing. **Romaine Lettuce**, the basis of a Caesar salad, is a taller, more conical group of leaves. My favourite is **Boston Lettuce**, often called Bibb and Butterhead. These plants are delicate and not very large. Hydroponic systems are used to grow wonderful Bibb Lettuce. **Summer Crisp** is like a combination of head Lettuce and leaf Lettuce. They produce loose heads of crisp, wrinkled leaves. The **Iceberg** type are the tight heads of Lettuce that are so often used in "house salads".

🍅 **Bolting** is a term used to describe the flowering activity of a plant. Once Lettuce forms a central stalk, it is the indicator that flower stalks are about to form and the plant is bitter tasting. Heat and inconsistent moisture levels will encourage premature bolting. There are some varieties of Crisphead Lettuce which are heat tolerant, try **Nevada**, **Micha** or **Canasta**.

🍅 Lettuce does not need a great deal of water, a popular misconception. What produces great, mild Lettuce is consistent watering and rapid growth. The soil therefore should be very fertile and rich in humus or compost. These types of organic soils will hold moisture for longer periods of time. Bitter Lettuce is often caused by water problems.

🍅 **Lettuce seeds must have light to germinate**, so do not cover the seeds when you sow them. I find that early-sown Lettuce produces the best as it germinates and starts life in cooler weather. If you are planning successive Lettuce crops, space your sowing about 10 days apart. It is wise to consider some shade for later season crops.

🍅 Companions for the Lettuce patch are easily found. Lettuce is particularly good with Garlic, Onions and plants of this family. Aphids will also be deterred if Chives are close by. Garlic, Radishes and Carrots make excellent bed buddies for Bibb Lettuce and all of the leaf Lettuce varieties.

Radicchio and other Chicory

Radicchio Palla rossa precoce, wow how's my Italian? This is the handle given to a plant that is really great to grow and eat, Radicchio or Chicory. Maybe you have noticed some dark red-purplish leaves in a mixed salad, with a white midrib . . . most likely this was it. Grow from seed sown indoors two months before the last frost date in your region, or directly outdoors about 14 days before the last frost days. In most of Canada that is mid-May for outdoor sowing. Although the heat of summer can cause Radicchio to be bitter, it is hard to beat. If you garden in a region that has long, protracted autumns, sow Radicchio in mid-summer and start to harvest in the cool days of October. In very mild regions, winter crops are not uncommon. I mulched my puny spring crop, one year, under a heavy blanket of leaves. The following spring, there they were, a bit bedraggled, but growing. My harvest was delicious.

Endive comes in several forms, but all are Chicory. Belgian Endive is the rather elongated, light-green bunched-leaf variety that has a somewhat bitter flavour. Bitterness is the hallmark of this gang if they are grown in warm weather. Like the Radicchio, Endives and **Escarole (*Chicorium endivia*)** prefer the cool, moist conditions of spring. Fertilizers are not generally recommended if the soil is very fertile and has a high organic matter content. I add compost and steer manure to most areas where leafy crops are to be grown.

Escarole and Endive are just different forms of the same plant, *Chicorium endivia*. Escarole is said to be the more frost tolerant of the two and sports larger, flat leaves. Endive is rather ragged looking and, in my opinion, a great garnish or display green.

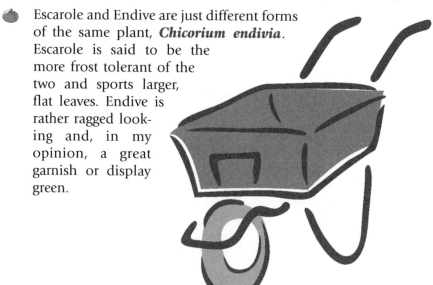

Rhubarb – Spring Tonic!

Nothing spells spring like the emergence of the **Rhubarb**. With almost magical stealth, this harbinger of the garden season doubles in size every day. I have a marvelous Rhubarb plant at the entrance way to my front garden. In my zone, there are limited plants which have large, coarse foliage so the Rhubarb fills the bill nicely. Mind you, they require a lot of room, so plant them wisely, they will shade out almost everything in their vicinity.

Rhubarb enjoys a rich, well-composted soil. Manure, manure tea and extra compost in spring and fall are suggested. I grow my Rhubarb in full sun and in a location that gets lots of water. It is not necessary to give them a lot of water all the time, but consistently moist is good.

The **leaves of Rhubarb** contain high concentrations of **oxalic acid**. This is poisonous to humans, so Grandma was correct when she told you to eat only the rosy red stems, dipped in sugar. Harvesting can begin in year three on a newly planted crown of Rhubarb. The stems are best pulled away from the plant, rather than cutting them off. Remove the leaves and shred them for the compost and store the stems in a cool, dark location until needed.

Rhubarb can be divided once the plants are too large, or over 10 years old. The roots are well established and will go down a long way, so division is not for the weak of back. In the late summer, slice through the crown of the plant with a sharpened spade. Prepare the new site with good, composted soil and manure. Fill the hole with water and plant the division into the water. Once the hole appears empty, start to back fill with good soil and water again. Wait at least one season before you harvest from this plant.

Spring tonics can utilize Rhubarb stems among other early spring plants. Most of us have experienced the rather cathartic effects of too much Rhubarb! Indeed, it is a gentle but powerful laxative, but also an astringent, which has the opposite affects. Centuries ago, Rhubarb was used in China and throughout Asia for its medicinal properties. I prefer it stewed or baked into delicious pies.

Peter Piper's Peppers

Peppers enjoy as much heat as you can give them during the growing season. Oddly enough, it is the temperature variation that encourages better blooms and, therefore, more fruit. I grow Peppers of all sorts in a **black plastic mulch**. This attracts the summer heat and keeps the soil almost too warm for other plants. The water flows down into the planting depressions in the plastic, ensuring each Pepper is well watered. What I've just learned is that Peppers prefer a cool jolt before transplanting.

Seed for Peppers is started indoors under almost tropical conditions. Warm soil, humid atmosphere and, once germinated, strong light. In my region of the country, artificial light is absolutely essential for 12 to 16 hours a day. Start the seeds about two months before the last frost date in spring. If you plant on the 24th of May weekend, then sow the seed around the last week of March. Transplant into 4" (10 cm) pots as soon as the first set of true leaves appear and lower the soil temperature to 70°F (21°C) and 10 degrees (6°C) lower at night. Lower the night temperatures once again by 10 degrees (6°C) once there are three sets of leaves on your Peppers. Finish your plants and ready them for outdoor planting at 70°F (21°C) day and night.

Peppers can be planted in rows or blocks as long as, when they are mature, they are just touching each other. Carrots and Peas are great buddies for Peppers, or just more Peppers works well for me. I have grown **"Big Bertha"** and had great success with her, a very large, Green Pepper with lots of fruit.

Capsaicin is the product within Peppers that is responsible for the "heat". Incidentally, **capsaicin is an excellent contact poison** for soft-bodied insects like aphids and Loopers. The heat in peppers is measured against a scale measured in Scoville units. Pure capsaicin rates at 15.5 million units; Bell Peppers rank at 0 and Jalapeños at 5,000; Thai Peppers rate upwards of 100,000 units, Habañeros (Scotch Bonnets) range from 100,000 to 300,000.

Red sweet Peppers are sweeter than Green sweet Peppers and Red hot Peppers are hotter than the green hot. Most Green Peppers will eventually turn red if left to ripen, however, by picking Peppers when green, the **plants continue to produce more fruit**. All Peppers prefer to be grown in rich, fertile soil with ample amounts of water. I have not grown them in containers on balconies or patios, but they should perform well in a good sunny spot, in a clay pot.

Relishing Cucumbers – Is Bigger Better?

- Cukes are a super plant to introduce children to gardening and the wonder of plants. A great deal can be taught about the birds and the bees, too, if one desires. Cucumbers are vines, as simple as that. No matter how much genetic work has been performed on them, they still want to scramble. Why not try them on a trellis or running up a grid? You will find that the fruit (the Cukes) will be straighter and less likely to be damaged by our friends the slugs.

- **Cukes like warm feet to germinate**, so cover the enriched soil, two weeks before planting, with black poly. They can be started indoors, but use Peat pots that can be planted as Cukes dislike any root disturbance. I have not had great success with Cucumbers indoors. Traditionally, they are planted in slight mounds with about five seeds per hill. Once germinated, they require consistent moisture to help prevent bitter fruit. There are **"bitterless"** varieties on the market; try **Aria**, **Jazzer** or **Holland** if you can find them.

- Cucumber Beetles are attracted to the bitter substance produced in the skin of the Cuke. Rather than spray, as Beetles are hard to kill anyway, grow the plants with even moisture, particularly after flowers are formed. This helps keep the Cukes mild. Even moisture levels will rid your crop of mutant-looking and strong-tasting fruit. **Do not plant Cukes near Pumpkins**, Squash or, in particular, Zucchini. They love to intermingle and the resulting offspring are neither Cuke nor Zucc.

- Cucumbers are best when picked and eaten fresh. The smaller fruit are usually crisp and the best tasting. These are often difficult to find as they seem to magically explode overnight. A good rule to follow is, if you think that the Cuke is almost big enough, don't wait, pick it. **Yellow skin is your clue that the cucumber is overripe**, these make excellent compost! Cucumber peelings are an old-fashioned remedy for ants. Apparently, if peelings were strewn across a door threshold, the ants would turn and move in the opposite direction.

- Slugs like the Cucumber patch a great deal. Of course it is cooler under the canopy of leaves and the soil is moist. Often, Cuke gardeners will mulch as well, offering five-star accommodations for these molluscs. **Wood ash** is the best material to spread around the Cukes. It provides much enjoyed Potassium for the plants and **slugs will not cross a banding of ashes**.

Very Berry

Around our garden, Raspberries are guarded as if they were heritage material or on the endangered species list. Enjoying the rather alkaline soil that constitutes the bulk of my garden, these ever-productive canes hold a mighty position in full sun. Raspberries are not particularly attractive landscape specimens, and they require **regular pruning to stay producing**. In the spring, the canes are cleaned of those that did not survive the winter and generally tidied up. I incorporate well-rotted or composted manure and cultivate.

Watering consistency is not as particular with Raspberries as with many other small fruits. I have a weeping hose that just trickles water at the soil surface. A high percentage of humus in the soil ensures the moisture is retained.

The Raspberry diet is easy, they like Potassium. Whether you use a commercially prepared granular product or a soluble one, apply twice a growing season at least, when the flowers are forming and then again after the canes are reduced in size in the autumn. Potassium helps many of the woodier-stemmed fruits as it promotes strong stalks and enhances fruit and seed development. Potassium is always the last number in a fertilizer ration N:P:K.

Strawberries are almost a science unto themselves. There are ever-bearing, day-neutral, June-bearing, the list is extending annually. All have a few cultural similarities no matter what they are called, one being the amount of water they enjoy. **Strawberries must be kept moist** to plump the berries, but water the plants overhead in the morning only. Plants which go into the evening with moist foliage are bound to get diseased. Berries like to be mulched as soon as the first flowers are formed. Use straw (the historic mulch), dry grass clippings, shredded bark or plastic sheeting.

One grower that produces a great crop of Strawberries uses a fertilizer formula rich in seaweed. The soluble components are 10-52-17 and the seaweed is 2-5-2. He swears that the addition of a surfactant or **soil-wetting agent is the key**. Try this yourself and always amend the planting soil with bone meal, blood meal and dig in ample amounts of compost or composted steer manure. Offsets can be removed from the mother plants as soon as they have formed a solid rosette of leaves. They root rapidly in moist, humid conditions.

Melons, Gourds and Garden Goliaths

Have you ever entered a giant Pumpkin contest? Well, I have not but I have entered Pumpkins in a fall fair. As a youngster, I always had a **"punkin" patch**, with at least one prospective prize winner tucked away. My uncle, a physician, suggested to me that I surgically feed my Pumpkin with milk. Apparently this was a surefire method of producing the largest specimen. Armed with old intravenous apparatus and plastic tubing patched into the stems of my crop, I fed them whole milk and waited, drawing plans for a Cinderella coach. Well, the milk soured, the Pumpkin grew huge, but I did not win the prize. A local judge deemed my entry disqualified as he felt it was a "field Squash" and not a Pumpkin. Not that this has affected me, at least so my therapist says . . . I have not grown Pumpkins since.

Muskmelons are the bowling-ball-sized melons with the Papaya-orange interiors. Their skin is smooth and thin with what appears to be a beige netting over it. **Cantaloupe**, as we often call them, are not the same plants. I think we inadvertently changed the name because "musk" has an unpleasant twang to it. Nevertheless, both melons are heat lovers and will produce in the northern regions of the country with a little help. Start seeds indoors, under lights, about a month before the outside planting date. Warm the outside soil with black plastic and cover the transplants with a cloche.

Watermelons, Muskmelons and, actually, all the members of this family prefer rich, composted soils. Dig in ample amounts of old manure or compost from leaves and grass clippings. As well, some agricultural lime or bone meal will help keep the pH high (alkaline). The plants require moderate watering from germination to the hardened-off stage. **Dry the transplants out for about a week** prior to planting outdoors. This strengthens the root system and reduces shock. Mulch and keep them moderately moist until the fruit is sized, then almost no water as the fruit ripens.

Northern gardeners may wish to reduce the number of fruits forming on the vine to a select few. **Watermelons** can get to be quite a size if only a couple are left to ripen. If possible, try and plant heritage seed melons. These older varieties have been around since the early 1900s and often are sweeter than the newer varieties.

A close friend of mine, and a good gardener to boot, decided to let a large Pumpkin scramble across the roof of her garage. Although it looked interesting, I had my doubts whether it would amount to much at all. Needless to say, I was wrong, the **"Roof Pumpkin"** as it became to be known, did not roll off the steep-pitched roof, it ripened and made great pies. Never underestimate the Melons, Gourds or Squash, they are capable of great and mighty feats. Growing these scramblers on trellises or obelisks is possible, however, the forming fruit needs to be supported with a netting or some such device.

Gourds, Zucchini and Squash could not be left off the list of "try once . . . if you dare" section. Once again, these plants offer a great boost to the uninitiated gardener, child or wanna-be horticulturist. Gourds offer the widest selection with Squash closing in at second place. **Zucchini, well what can one say?** You know that you are really not approachable if you have to buy Zucchini at the supermarket during growing season. Everybody seems to have bushels to give away. Gourds, once dried and waxed, make curious botanical oddities for the Thanksgiving table while the Squash end up either as a vegetable side dish or a pie. Goodness knows there is probably a Zucchini or two in the turkey stuffing, and always in the chocolate cake for dessert.

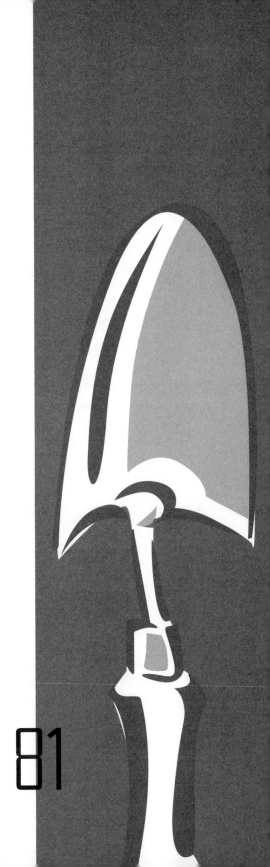

INSIDE OUT

houseplants

81

House-Pests

Aphids abound on houseplants in the late days of summer. As the day length reduces, it seems that their activity increases. The key to effective control is diligent application, **every 10 days**, of insecticidal soap products. If you prefer to use a chemical product, follow a similar regime.

Flame of the Woods
– a Hot Houseplant

Ixora coccinea, or **Flame of the Woods**, requires rather good light, like that from a western exposure or southern window. The soil mixture should be very rich in compost or humus, yet well drained. Ixora have rather sensitive roots systems, therefore be cautious with fertilizers. I recommend that you reduce the suggested rate by half and feed them regularly. You may consider using cold tea as a supplement, as well. The acidity of the tannins in the tea will benefit the **Ixora**.

People of the Amazon basin utilize many species of Ixora for its medicinal properties. The beautiful *Ixora coccinea* is used to make a medication for **ear infections**. I would prefer to just enjoy the blossoms rather than boiling them up in a tea. After all, it takes a certain amount of encouragement to get them to bloom in the first place.

A long time ago, I had the opportunity to visit the Dominican Republic on a vacation. The hotel complex that we stayed at was relatively new, without much finished landscaping. One cheery morning I heard the "jardinieres" singing. Interested, I stepped over to see what they were up to. They were planting a hedge row of Ixora. The soil was the worst I have seen and the plants in full wilt. My experience told me that they would never make a hedge. Well, to my surprise, within the 10 days that I was vacationing the darn things rooted and bloomed. Is there no justice?

Old Fashioned but Still Winners – Calceolaria and Cineraria

- Calceolaria are often referred to as the **"Slipper Flower"** because of their interesting pouch-like flowers. For the most part the blooms are in the orange-red tones, often with speckles and spots on the pouches. The leaves of this plant are rather tissue-like and remind me of Primula. This kind of leaf is also the favourite hunting ground for whiteflies, so watch out!

- **Calceolaria require fairly bright light** but they enjoy cooler temperatures. If you have a sunroom or an area in the house that is a bit cooler than the other rooms, this is the ideal spot for the Calceolaria. The soil or medium that they are growing in does not like to become dry between waterings, yet they do not like to sit in a tray of water.

- **Cineraria**, appear to have hundreds of small, daisy-like blooms on them. The colours are rather odd in combination, almost as if a primary school child decided to test out their new markers. Red and white, blue and white, off-tones of blue, purple, pink and even maroon. Conditions for these rather **Victorian plants** are identical to that of the Calceolaria; cool and in bright sun.

Easter Lily – Hardy or Not?

- If you are getting an **Easter Lily** this year, look for a specimen that has a good straight stem, at least five flower buds, with three buds unopened. The yellow pollen that is on the anthers inside the white flower will stain skin and clothing severely, so be careful! Some growers and retailers remove the pollen in an attempt to increase the longevity of the bloom; I prefer them to be intact . . . but that is just personal taste.

- Easter Lilies will overwinter in climates as cold as in Canadian Prairie gardens, and bloom the following year. I have had a number of callers inform me of what they thought was a near miracle . . . an **Easter Lily in full bloom, outdoors, in Saskatchewan**. However, it would be a wise gardener who plants the Lilies close to the house, or at least in a protected area of the garden.

Boston Ferns enjoy a Tea Party

🌿 Boston Ferns, as well as other tropical Ferns, enjoy **excessive humidity**. The Canadian home in winter is not an ideal locale for these specimens. Try placing them in a large clear plastic bag for a few days, with ample mist . . . this increases the humidity to a range that they enjoy.

🌿 If you are planning to use Boston Ferns in planters, to hang on the porch or even to **plant in the shade** of your secret garden, purchase new plants. The Ferns that you have coddled along indoors for the winter season (all 11 months of it!) tend to do poorly out of doors. Freshly purchased Ferns will also show signs of adjustment, but do not usually succumb to the weather.

🌿 Boston Ferns are most often sold in hanging baskets. Their lush foliage and stringy rootlets usually fall over the sides and hang beautifully. The planting mixture is likely light and predominantly Peat Moss, causing it to dry very rapidly. **The quickest way to lose a Boston Fern is to allow it to dry out.** I like to treat mine to the last cup(s) of cold tea after dinner. The slight acidity of the tea is beneficial, as is the extra moisture.

🌿 The stringy, hairlike threads on a Boston Fern are actually root-like structures. They will form new rosettes of Fern, much like Quack Grass will form new plants. I like to wind the threads around the edge of the pot and pin them into place with a small staple of wire. In a matter of weeks, new Ferns are forming. You can remove the new plants or allow them to stay and fill up the container.

🌿 Old Boston Ferns tend to have **woody centres** and long, insipid foliage. This marks the time to divide and conquer. Remove the Fern from its container and shake off as much of the planting medium as possible. Using a sharp knife, slice the main crown into quarters or even smaller. Each clump can now be replanted, to the same depth, in fresh humus soil. Water with a good transplant fertilizer and tent the whole pot in a clear plastic bag. This will increase the humidity and encourage new fronds. Remove the plant from the plastic once there is evidence of new growth.

🌿 *Dolichos lablab* **'Ruby Moon'** should be grown for its name alone. This fascinating climber sports Sweet Pea-like flowers that eventually form enormous, brown seed pods. The pods offer an unusual effect as they are flanked by deep greenish-purple foliage. Considered a half-hardy perennial, the *Dolichos* could be over-wintered indoors.

The Angels of Scent –
Brugmansia and Datura

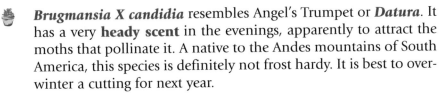 *Brugmansia X candidia* resembles Angel's Trumpet or **Datura**. It has a very **heady scent** in the evenings, apparently to attract the moths that pollinate it. A native to the Andes mountains of South America, this species is definitely not frost hardy. It is best to over-winter a cutting for next year.

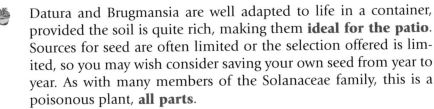 Datura and Brugmansia are well adapted to life in a container, provided the soil is quite rich, making them **ideal for the patio**. Sources for seed are often limited or the selection offered is limited, so you may wish consider saving your own seed from year to year. As with many members of the Solanaceae family, this is a poisonous plant, **all parts**.

Seeds of many plants can have a very tough outer coat. In the case of Datura and Brugmansia, the outer shell should be treated to enhance germination. You can **use a nail file to score the end** of each seed, or roll the seeds on fine sandpaper to roughen up the surface. An overnight soaking will soften the seed coat and start the germination process. In most of temperate North America, the seed is started indoors in February for bloom outdoors in August.

Furry Fern Feet

The common name(s) for Davallia range from perhaps the best-known Rabbit's Foot Fern, to Squirrel's Foot Fern, referring to the hairy rhizomes by which the plant regenerates. ***Davallia fijiensis* (Rabbit's Foot Fern)** has a stout rhizome with scales and very long amber-coloured hairs.

Davallia grown on moss poles or the black fern bark supports tend to climb and twine themselves around quite attractively. Classroom specimens are best grown this way so that the students can observe the habit of the rhizomes and, if allowed, brush and groom the hair.

All Davallia require very good humidity, particularly during their growing period. You will find that most species require a dormant period sometime over the winter. It is most common to see ***D. fijiensis* sleep from December until March**. Sleep refers to the lack of new growth and perhaps the discarding of older back fronds. ***D. canariensis*** and other species that come from hot dry climates will rest for a six-week period in the summertime.

The soil mixture for Davallia is best kept more acidic than most. This is accomplished by mixing liberal amounts of compost, Peat Moss or coconut fibre with a rich potting soil. I use three parts organic matter to one part soil. The mixture should not dry out during the growing period, however, while in dormancy the plant doesn't require as much moisture. Feed frequently with a good soluble fertilizer high in Potassium (the last number in the ratio).

Indoor Herbs

Garlic makes a rather unusual but practical houseplant. Simply remove the papery covering of the cloves and plant several in a small pot of rich potting medium. Allow the green, Onion-like sprouts to reach 4 to 6" (10-15 cm) in height before cutting. Garlic greens are wonderful in winter salads.

If you want to try growing Basil indoors for winter culinary delights, try ***Ocimum basilicum minimum* (Spicy Globe Basil)**. It is a flavourful, dense, compact 8-10" (20-25 cm) plant. Plant in a pot with good drainage, water thoroughly when the soil is dry and fertilize weekly. Keep in a sunny window.

Orchids - Queen of the Flowers

🌿 Orchids are, for the most part, very easily grown indoors. Many species are **grown in coarse bark or similar media**. They should be watered often and placed in strong sunlight for the best results. High Nitrogen feeds are also encouraged.

🌿 One of the easiest Orchid groups to grow in the home are the **Moth Orchids or Phalaenopsis**. They tend to have large flowers borne on a gracefully arching spike. The flowers can last six months or more under good conditions. Often, once the blossoms are finished, a secondary growth occurs on the stalk. This little baby is known as a **Kiki**.

🌿 Orchids belong to a wide and very diverse family, touted as being the largest and of the oldest. I am confident that this family has some of the most interesting plants that I have seen. Many flowers resemble insects, and actually mimic pheromonal scents to attract male insects. These poor, deceived fellows attempt to mate with the imposter flower and, in the process, pollinate it with pollen from another orchid. This teasing is one way that the Orchids regenerate and hybridize for survival.

🌿 One of the best ways to learn about, and eventually acquire Orchids, is to **attend a local orchid show** and sale. Here you will meet enthusiasts at all levels of development. Caution is advised for the first few visits as you will be overwhelmed at the diversity of colour and shapes of these beauties. Generally, there are many plants for sale in various stages of growth. A good idea is to start with a plant in bud, this way you will likely see results faster.

🌿 **Many Orchids are epiphytic**, which means they live on other plants. The growing medium for these kinds of Orchids is a mixture of bark chips, coarse Perlite® and, often, tree fern shreddings and a host of highly organic and chunky materials. This mix is so porous that the water runs over the roots and drains off quickly, just like it might if the orchid lived in a tree. It is therefore necessary to **fertilize the Orchid regularly** and with a high-Nitrogen feed. The decomposing organic matter requires extra Nitrogen as a fuel.

Prickly Situations – Cacti and Their Friends

- Cacti and many other succulent plants require particular care during the winter months. Most of these arid-loving specimens are **accustomed to a dry winter dormancy**. To achieve the desired results at home, all but cease watering, eliminate fertilizing and lower the night temperatures, if possible.

- Cacti are perennials which bear spine cushions and can withstand drought because of their succulent stems or bodies. Some plants which are called Cacti are actually succulents, their leaves as well as stems store moisture.

- True Cacti are indigenous only to northern, central and southern America and neighbouring islands. Some species have been introduced to the "Old World" and have gone wild, leading people to believe they are native species.

- Cacti require a rather long rest, starting in November and ending in April. They require no fertilizer and reduced water. Blooming species such as the **Christmas Cactus** delight in cooler temperatures, lower light, as well as reduced water. Once blooming ceases, resume normal culture.

- Tequila, a Mexican liquor, is made from the **Agave** plant. This noble desert dweller is armed much like the Cacti it lives with, however, it is a member of the Lily family. Fabrics, food, drink and art are all made from this versatile plant.

- Typical Cacti have **spines which are actually modified leaves**. It is the style and arrangement of these spines that help determine the species of the Cactus. As in many sciences, there are exceptions to the rule. The **Epiphyllum**, or **Orchid Cactus**, does not have spines and its close cousins the **Zygocactus**, or **Christmas Cactus**, is smooth also.

- Cacti enjoy a long winter's nap without food and very little water. In Canada, the light starts to reduce in October and starts to increase again in March. The times between are slow for Cacti. Never feed them with a Nitrogen fertilizer and, during this time, limit their water. They will most likely shrivel somewhat as a result of this diet. During high light, re-establish watering practices and they will plump back up, and most likely sprout new growth.

The **Saguaro Cactus** that is so typical in western movies is a very stately Cactus. I would not recommend attempting to grow one indoors, and **absolutely never "borrow" one from the desert**. These plants are all protected under law, and are sacred to the local Pima Indians in the Sonoran Desert. Apparently, this "old man cactus" takes 80 years before he even grows his first arm, so imagine how old some of these specimens must be.

Christmas, **Easter** and **Thanksgiving Cactus**, are the topic of many discussions. The most commonly asked questions deal with the stubborn attitude these plants have towards blooming. My suggestion is to grow them outdoors during fine weather. Feed them heavily with a high-Potassium feed such as 10-10-27 and water them often. This diet will force a lot of nice new growth. When frost is apparent, bring them indoors and stop feeding at once. Reduce the watering so as to cause the foliage to wrinkle. Place the plant in a location where it will get cooler night temperatures. Leave it alone and it should bloom.

Aloe barbadensis is often used in the home to soothe minor burns and skin inflammations. This fleshy-stemmed member of the Lily family prefers a well-draining soil containing equal parts of soil and Perlite®. They respond well to bone meal and strong light.

Aloe Vera is not a cactus at all, it is really a member of the Lily family. This fleshy-leaved specimen produces a beautiful flower resembling tiny coral bells fixed to a long, slender stalk. Like Cacti, this plant prefers a dry winter season.

Potted Primrose and other spring perennials are delightful indoors in the early spring. Primroses offer a delicate, sweet scent as well as a riot of brightly coloured flowers. Remember, these spring beauties **prefer cooler temperatures** and dislike drying out.

Coffee can make a great houseplant if you have relatively good sunlight. The glossy leaves are even greener if they are fed with a fertilizer rich in Potassium like 10-10-27. *Coffea arabica* is the botanical handle for the plant that produces the Beans used by commerce. There is a dwarf form **'Nana'** which can produce the typical fragrant flowers at a height of only 2' (60 cm).

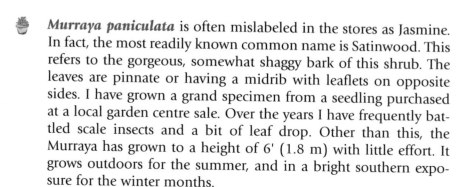 *Murraya paniculata* is often mislabeled in the stores as Jasmine. In fact, the most readily known common name is Satinwood. This refers to the gorgeous, somewhat shaggy bark of this shrub. The leaves are pinnate or having a midrib with leaflets on opposite sides. I have grown a grand specimen from a seedling purchased at a local garden centre sale. Over the years I have frequently battled scale insects and a bit of leaf drop. Other than this, the Murraya has grown to a height of 6' (1.8 m) with little effort. It grows outdoors for the summer, and in a bright southern exposure for the winter months.

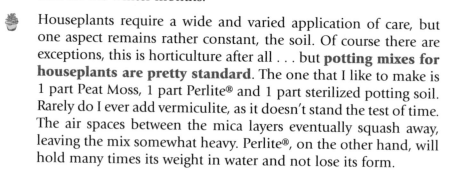 Houseplants require a wide and varied application of care, but one aspect remains rather constant, the soil. Of course there are exceptions, this is horticulture after all . . . but **potting mixes for houseplants are pretty standard**. The one that I like to make is 1 part Peat Moss, 1 part Perlite® and 1 part sterilized potting soil. Rarely do I ever add vermiculite, as it doesn't stand the test of time. The air spaces between the mica layers eventually squash away, leaving the mix somewhat heavy. Perlite®, on the other hand, will hold many times its weight in water and not lose its form.

Stubborn Bloomers – Words of Encouragement

Lipstick plants have been known to be "stubborn" in the blooming department. To encourage these colourful hanging basket plants into bloom; reduce the amount of water they get; use a 10-60-10 fertilizer ratio and do not repot them. Often, under this regime, they'll produce a great many blossoms in February.

Calla Lilies are very popular outdoor container plants in Canada. These attractive, bulbous plants must be brought indoors for the winter. Callas may be stored moist and dark or kept growing year round. The bulbs must not dry out completely during dormancy, and require light fertilizing and moderate sun if you intend to keep them growing.

Hoya carnosa and its many relatives often grow beautifully and forget to bloom. I think that many growers treat their Hoya plants too well. The plants like to be in a tight pot, and I always grow mine in terra cotta. Remembering that this genus comes from an area of the world where the seasons are wet and dry, not hot and cold like here, the Hoya should be dried sufficiently between waterings in an attempt to mimic this condition. Next, they respond well to high Phosphorus and Potassium fertilizers. The ratio should have higher middle and last numbers than the first. I give my plants a spring tonic of 2 tbsp. (30 mL) **Epsom salts** in 1 quart (1 L) of water. This tonic seems to boost the fertilizer's abilities. **Never fertilize a dry soil**, always water first, then feed.

Hoya blossoms are borne on a flower stalk. This appendage is not unlike a fruiting spur on an Apple tree. Some people remove this stalk and that is the end of the blossoms for some time. The stalk extends with each successive flowering adding a bit of tissue. If you have to apply an insecticide or soap product, try to avoid this part of the plant. It is delicate tissue and burns easily.

Clivia miniata, or **Kafir Lily**, makes a striking houseplant and exotic summer patio specimen. You might as well get as much use out of it as possible, they have become rather expensive lately. The leaves are what I enjoy the most. As if from an Egyptian painting, they originate in the centre and arch on opposite sides as huge strap-like tongues. Each new set of leaves fits into the previous so the plant has a pleated look. Oh yes, **the flower is gorgeous**, when it appears! Orange tubular structures are borne in a whorl atop a solid stem, held high above the majestic foliage.

So Now What do I do with This Gift?

- **Poinsettia plants** are the mainstay of the Christmas holiday season. If you are encouraging last year's plant into colour for this season, there is a rather tedious process. They must be placed in a dark place for at least 14 hours a day, and then in strong sunlight for the remaining 10. This bedtime procedure should start in October to ensure colour for December.

- The spent flowers of the huge and exotic **Amaryllis** should be removed, as well as the hollow stems. The strap-like leaves most likely require support and should be left to grow on. The plant requires good light, soluble 10-10-27 fertilizer and frequent watering to size the bulb for next year's explosion of blooms.

- **Amaryllis** which bloomed over the New Year may be past their prime by February. Remove the old flowers and their stalks, but **leave the leaves** to grow. Place the plant in good sunlight, feed with a high-Potassium feed and stake it. Wait until spring to plant outdoors, they perform wonderfully well.

- *Ficus benjamina*, or **Weeping Fig** of the trade, are notorious for leaf drop. In low-light periods they are apt to drop a great many leaves. Take caution not to overwater during this apparent pouty period. They will recover and produce new, smaller foliage once they adjust to the current light conditions.

- **Azaleas are popular holiday potted plants** in the spring, for Easter and Mother's Day. Although they are lush and loaded with flowers when you buy them, in the home they often drop blooms and then foliage. The reason is that Azaleas are **cool-loving plants** and require excessively high humidity. Think of British Columbia outside in the spring, this is an ideal climate for Azaleas.

- Florist Azaleas can be kept alive indoors and, sometimes, coaxed into bloom again. Some of my viewers plant their Azalea gifts outdoors in semi-shade for the summer months. The option exists to plant, pot and all, or amend the soil so as to make it very acidic. Buds for the following year are set in the cool autumn days, just before heavy frost. **The trick is to allow the buds to set, not freeze** the plant, and get it back indoors before the snow flies. Others just leave them alone indoors, never let them dry out, and they bloom in spite of it all.

Florist Hydrangeas are popular gift plants in the early spring. They have huge, basketball-sized flowers in pink, blue and white. If you garden in a climate that is warmer than zone 4 USDA, these plants can be wintered outdoors. In cooler regions, they are best enjoyed during the spring holidays and not regarded as permanent garden plants.

The fascinating *Aechmea fasciata* or **Silver Vase Plant** is quite a novelty. The tall, vase-shaped, rough leaves appear to be dusted with a whitish powder. Out of the centre grows a pineapple-like, neon-pink bract with purple bead flowers. This Bromeliade requires water in the centre of the vase and relatively high humidity. Once the pink bract has passed, **the mother plant will not bloom again**. However, the progeny it produces at the base can be removed, potted and in time they will bloom. To encourage blooms on young plants, place a couple of Apple cores or whole Apples near the plant and seal the entire plant in a clear plastic bag. The Apples give off natural ethylene gas which encourages blooms.

Chrysanthemums from the florist shop make excellent, long-lasting gift plants. Once planted out into the garden, they may not perform quite as well. In temperate areas of North America, the florists' variety mum will root in and overwinter to produce flowers the following autumn. This strain of mum sets its flower buds as the days get shorter. In colder regions, the buds may form but often they are frozen before they have a chance to open.

Palms have a great tendency to tip burn. Much literature suggests that this is caused by excessive salt build up in the soil. To a degree I believe this to be so, but the worst culprit is lack of humidity. There is not a great deal we can do in the house to increase the humidity to the percentage that most Palms will like. The chemicals that are added to make our water potable also play a role in tip burn. **I end up trimming the tips with scissors**.

Dieffenbachia plants are known for their ability to constrict the throat if ingested, and they also are notorious for dropping lower leaves. Often the beautiful plant that you selected in the store, once settled in your home, will drop most of its bottom leaves. The resulting form resembles something from a cartoon comic. This abrupt reaction is just an adjustment to lower light and a different climate. If you are not happy with the "new" appearance of the plant, install another twining plant in the same pot. It will scramble up the naked trunk and fill in the void.

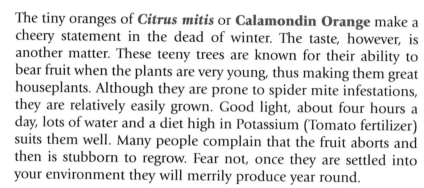 Gloxinia are those grand, fuzzy-leafed Gesneriades that almost everyone's grandparents grew indoors. They have never really fallen from favour as a good and reliable houseplant. Gesneriades is the family name for plants that belong to the African Violet group. **Gloxinia** have a large tuber-like root that actually resembles a Begonia. They are most often purchased in bloom and remain in this state for several months. During lower light periods they tend to grow a bit weak and look like they are tired. In this case, put them to bed in a warm, dark, dry area for a couple of months, at least. After bedtime, place them back in diffused light and they will begin to sprout again. **Cold tea is an excellent tonic** for these bulbous beauties.

The tiny oranges of *Citrus mitis* or **Calamondin Orange** make a cheery statement in the dead of winter. The taste, however, is another matter. These teeny trees are known for their ability to bear fruit when the plants are very young, thus making them great houseplants. Although they are prone to spider mite infestations, they are relatively easily grown. Good light, about four hours a day, lots of water and a diet high in Potassium (Tomato fertilizer) suits them well. Many people complain that the fruit aborts and then is stubborn to regrow. Fear not, once they are settled into your environment they will merrily produce year round.

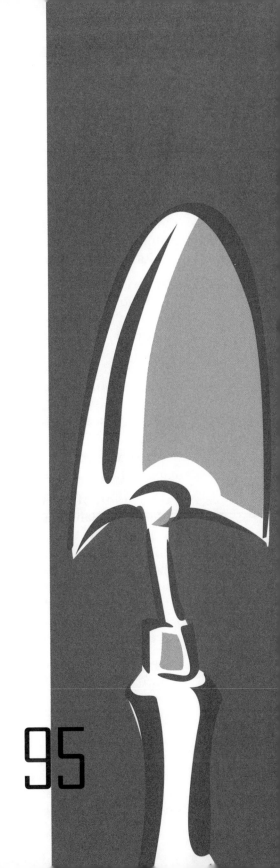

PROPAGATION

95

Seedy Characters

Columbine, or *Aquilegia*, set huge amounts of seed in early summer. If you wish to select varieties, gather the seed now and store it in sealed containers, medication bottles are ideal. **I store seeds in the crisper of the refrigerator** . . . labeled of course!

Coleus has enjoyed a revival in the shade garden over the past few years. These vibrant annuals can be grown from seed indoors fairly easily. The trick is to start early and provide them with bottom heat. Tiny seedlings may be transplanted once they have a couple of sets of true leaves. A wise gardener will treat the soil with a soluble fungicide prior to seeding.

To **pre-germinate seed**, place a piece of thick paper towelling in the bottom of a clean (preferably glass) container. Dampen the towelling with warm water and pour off any excess. Place the amount of seed to be pre-germinated on the moist towelling so that the seeds are not touching each other. It is a good idea to add about 20% extra seed to compensate for germination failure. Cover the container but not the seed with plastic wrap, and place on top of the refrigerator or in another dark and very warm location (85°F/30°C). Check the paper towelling regularly to ensure that it is moist, and mist with warm water if it is not. Once the seeds show signs of life (a tiny white, fuzzy root will appear) remove them individually and plant into sterile planting mix.

Propagation of Hyssop is usually by seed. I would start them in April for planting outdoors in late May or early June. Take all the general precautions for sowing seeds but pay particular attention and use No-Damp® to discourage the damping off disease. Once the seedlings are transplantable, and the soil is workable in your border, move them outdoors and plant them about 18" (45 cm) apart. In the early spring you can also make new plants by cuttings. With a sharp knife, simply remove a soft, top portion of the plant that has about three sets of leaves.

Large seeds such as **Castor Oil Bean** and **Datura** should be soaked in water overnight. This process softens the seed coat and promotes a speedier germination. These two plants should be started indoors in the month of February.

Impatiens are a delightful collection of shade-loving plants. Seeds sown in early January produce noble plants for May transplanting. Some species have asexual propagation restrictions due to genetic copyright issues. Plants raised from early sown seed are often ready for cuttings by the first part of summer.

- **Sweet Peas** are one of the easiest and most rewarding garden plants to grow. The seeds are large, enabling children and those with physical restrictions to handle them with ease, germination is rapid and flowers have an exquisite aroma. Sweet Peas make excellent cut flowers too.

- **Foxgloves** or **Digitalis** were the original source of the heart medication **Digoxin**. In the garden they warm the heart with their showy spikes of tubular bell flowers. These biennials require two seasons to mature, so plant seed and yearling transplants simultaneously to afford continuous blossom.

- To start **Datura** or **Brugmansia** seeds, I suggest that you soak them overnight in water. Knick or rasp a bit of the seed coat with a knife or your emery board. This will soften the tough seed coat, allowing the water to be absorbed. The following day, sow the seeds to a depth twice their diameter in warm, pre-moistened soil. Start them four to six weeks before the last frost date in your area.

Leave it up to the Leaves

- **Leaf cuttings** are among the easiest ways to propagate new plants from your favourites. The classic example is the tuberous or rhizomatous Begonia leaf. If you look at the underside of these Begonia leaves, you will see a very distinct venation. Score the larger veins with a very sharp utility knife or razor blade. Place the wounded leaf on a moistened bed of Peat Moss, scores down. It is a good idea to treat the mix with a fungicide before positioning the leaf. Place a small pebble or weight on the leaf to ensure that the wounded veins come in contact with the potting mix. Tent the entire arrangement under clear plastic until there is evidence of leaflets forming at the wounds. Under ideal conditions this should take about three weeks. **As Begonias prefer low light** conditions anyway, do not place the tented leaf in direct sunlight, it will cook. Once the new plants are established, and the old leaf decayed, remove the wee plants and pot them up. They will be identical to the parent.

❧ *Bryophyllum* or **Air Plant** is a popular plant in the botany classroom. This curious plant produces plantlets along the edge of each leaf. The common names implies that it will grow on air, a misconception at best. The tiny plantlets that form need to be potted in a well-draining media and receive water in order for them to establish properly.

❧ **African Violets** and the popular houseplant genus *Peperomia* are both propagated from **leaf cuttings**. These plants do not have to have a leaf stem attached in order to root, but commonly they are rooted with a stem attached. In both cases, the new plants form along the midrib of the leaf blade. **The rooting mixture must be porous** and well draining yet stable enough to support the leaf and developing plant. Pure Perlite® is often used as it is inert, sterile and will hold many times its weight in water without collapsing.

❧ *Sedum sp., Crassula argenta* or Jade Plant and many other **succulents root tremendously well from simply one leaf**. I suspect that this is an adaptation that has developed over time so that even in the harshest climates these plants can propagate. In order to make a nice, full-looking pot of Sedum, fill the surface with the tiny bead-shaped leaves. If you can't figure out which is top or bottom, lay each of them on their sides. They'll all root and fill the pot in no time. Tenting is not necessary for most succulent plants to root. **Expect to see some activity in a few weeks**.

❧ *Sanseveria trifasciata laurenti* is just the fancy botanical name for Snake Plant or **Mother-in-law's Tongue**. It is difficult to determine if this plant is all leaves or where the leaves end and the stem starts. Safe to say, it is propagated from leaves. The trick here is to ensure that the segments you cut off are marked to distinguish which is top and which is bottom. Rooting, of course, occurs on the bottom end of the cutting. What I do is make a notch in the top of the segment to tell me **"this end up"**. Rooting is very easy, just stick a segment about 2" (5 cm) in length into a well-draining medium. Water it or them in to reduce any air that may be in the mix and wait about three weeks. Roots will develop and new growth will appear from the base.

Asexual Propagation – Stem Cuttings

🌿 Dieffenbachia are the easiest plants to propagate using a stem cutting. Goodness knows that there is rarely a shortage of stem on these plants, the foliage is all at the top. Keep in mind that, where you cut the **Dieffenbachia**, it will produce several side shoots just below the wound, making the plant much bushier. The cord wood that is harvested can be cut into lengths that each have a couple of leaf scars. The scars appear as lighter rings, often with a teardrop-shaped bud apparent. Lay these segments lengthwise in a flat or container of moist Peat Moss. I like to tent or cover the flat with plastic to increase the humidity. Within a few weeks, there will be new growth starting at the site of the teardrop-shaped buds. Remove them, pot them, and you are in the business of Dieffenbachia farming.

🌿 *Pelargonium hortorum* or plain old-fashioned **Geraniums**, are classically reproduced from stem cuttings, often referred to as "slips". I was first introduced to propagation by stem cuttings when I was quite young. Family members all seemed to share "slips" and cultural techniques. In high school, during the winter months, certain teachers lined the broad window sills with hoards of the **slips** that they had taken prior to frost. One tip that has been valuable to me over the years is not to root the Geranium cuttings in water. Yes, I know that it does work, but the root system that is produced takes a longer time to develop in soil and is prone to fungal attacks. Allow the cuttings of Geranium to dry overnight so that the wound has a chance to form a skin. This little trick will reduce the common occurrence of black leg, a debilitating fungus.

🌿 Many trees and shrubs will root easily from stem cuttings. One such plant is the **Curly Willow** that is common in winter floral arrangements. Left in the container that it came in, it will often push roots to fill the vase. As Willows are naturally water-loving plants, keep them wet until you can plant them outside in the springtime. Provided you live in a region of the country that is above USDA zone 2, you'll have a new plant.

There are many different opinions on the type of cut or wound to make when taking a stem cutting. I recall quite the debate regarding the use of a **slanted cut versus a flush cut**. The reasoning offered had to do with the amount of surface area that would be exposed. Apparently, the more the better. In my opinion, the best cut is flush and taken just below a leaf scar or joint. It is at this point that there is the most cell activity, and it will probably produce the best rooting.

A great deal of confusion surrounds the when, where and what size of stem when it comes to cuttings. There are no hard and fast rules, but I follow a simple "common sense" approach. I **take cuttings from new wood that has just started to mature**. The thickness is generally no greater than a lead pencil and, if the foliage is quite large, I dock it by 50%. **Docking** is the removal of foliage to reduce the amount of transpiration or water loss. The leaves of a cutting are generally replaced anyway, so docking them should not concern you. Finally, rooting cuttings must have high humidity so I tent them in clear plastic.

Root Division – Long Division, Addition and Subtraction

Propagation of *Davallia fejeenis* or **Rabbit's Foot Fern** is successful by division or by layering a rhizome in a high organic content mix. I recommend that if you are rooting a piece away from the mother plant that you envelop the cutting and the pot in a large clear plastic bag. This will increase the much needed humidity during the rooting phase. Once new fronds start to appear you are assured that roots have formed. Cuttings are best taken during active growth.

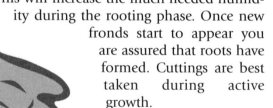

⚘ **"Root cutting"** is likely to be the least-used method of propagation in your garden, but it shouldn't be. Root cuttings are different from divisions in that smaller amounts of tissue are needed. It is critical to establish and mark the **proximal** (growing or crown end) of the root or the **distal** (the rooting) end. **Oriental Poppy,** *Papaver orientale* is easily propagated from a small root cutting. This is best done in the summer when the plant is basically dormant and the roots are full of nourishment from the spring season. Make a flush cut to mark the growing end of the root (proximal) and a slanted cut to mark the rooting end (distal). When it comes time to plant the cuttings you will know which end is up. A single root will form a perfect Poppy clump within a season or two.

⚘ The medium that is best suited for establishing good root cuttings is a mixture of sand and Peat Moss. The moss holds sufficient moisture and the sand provides good drainage. Plants with fine root systems may be propagated in Perlite® and Peat Moss mixtures, also. **Root cuttings develop side buds and new growth rapidly**, thus making this an easy method to increase your plant inventory.

⚘ Plants that lend themselves well to root cuttings are: Horseradish, Phlox, edible Figs, Bittersweet, Japanese Flowering Quince, Trumpet Vine, Devil's Walking Stick, Flowering Almond, many Rose species, Raspberry and Blackberry, Lilacs, Oriental Pears, Sumac, Poplar, Ferns, Daphne and Buckeye.

⚘ Many of us are more than familiar with **suckers** on Lilacs, Poplar, May Day Trees and Chokecherry. It is this part of the plant that is used to produce the root cuttings. Plants which have an over abundance of "suckers" are good candidates for this type of propagation. **Caution should be exercised** when considering Roses or other grafted material. The rootstalk is generally wild or species plants, grown for their tenacity and aggressiveness. Propagation of these plants, although easy, may not be rewarding.

Bulblets, Cormels
and Other Nursery Rhymes

Lilies have a type of bulb that appears to be made up of a series of scales. These individual segments can be removed from the mother bulb and planted in flats of rich, well-draining soil. Each of these scales will produce from three to five bulblets identical to the parent. This process is called **"scaling"** in the industry and is used to increase inventory of new varieties of Lilies very quickly. Try this procedure in the summer, just after the plants have flowered.

Bulbils, or aerial stem bulblets, are evident on many Lilies in the axils of the leaves. In particular, you will find these little gems on species such as *L. tigrinum*, the **Tiger Lily**, and *L. sargentiae*, **Sargent's Lily**. What actually happens is that tiny, dark spheres form several weeks after the flowers are past. The presence of these appendages often cause gardeners some distress as they look like a problem. The bulbils can be harvested shortly before they fall naturally, and can be planted that season. The following year a single leaf will form and a new bulb starts to develop.

Basal bulb cutting is the principal method of propagating the **Hyacinth**. The process is well worth trying, as you can produce a fair number of new plants from a single bulb. A mature bulb is harvested after the leaves yellow and die down. Three incisions are made with the blade of a sharp, straight knife across the base of the bulb. The cuts should be deep enough to **score the basal plate** and the growing point. You may wish to practise on a couple of bulbs to establish the appropriate depth. Dissect a bulb to determine how deep you should go. Dust the wounds with a good fungicide and place the bulbs in a flat of dry sand or soil for a couple of weeks, cut end down. The temperature to callus the wounds should be around 70°F (21°C). From here, the bulbs are cured in warm temperatures, about 10°F (6°C) higher, and in the dark with high humidity for about three months. Thereafter, plant the mother bulbs in nursery beds in the fall. The following spring, the bulblets produce an abundance of foliage and the new Hyacinths are ready to size.

- **Cormels are baby corms** and are actually not bulbs but swollen stem bases. **Gladiolus** are a good example of plants which have corms. Cormels are produced between the old and the new corms each year. One way to **increase the number of new cormels**, is to plant the corm only a few inches deep. Cormels tend to be tough little guys if they are removed and stored. Soaking them in water prior to planting will plump them up, or store them in moist Peat Moss over winter.

- **Tubers are swollen underground stems** that have the ability to store energy. The most common example is the Potato or Jerusalem Artichoke. **Dahlias** are not true tubers but tuberous roots. The only difference is that tubers have "eyes" or growing points along the entirety. Tuberous rooted plants have a top and a bottom, tubers are not specific. Propagation is easy for most tubers. It requires cutting the tuber to ensure that there are at least a couple of growing "eyes" to produce the stems and roots required.

Neo-Natal Intensive Care

- Cleanliness is not only next to Godliness, it is absolutely imperative if you are raising plants from seed. Many a "would-be seedsman" has lost his or her entire crop as a result of poor sanitation. Sterilized or pasteurized planting mixes are great, but if a pathogen is introduced, let's say from an unclean pot or flat, the disease runs rampant. **Resistance to pathogens is non-existent in these "ultra clean" environments.** I do encourage recycling of planting containers but they must be treated with household bleach before you plant.

- Cuttings, seedlings and all manner of new developing plant life require similar conditions: warmth in varying degrees; moisture, both in the planting mix and as humidity; light. Unfortunately, these conditions are excellent for many fungi, too. I always pretreat the mix with a liquid fungicide called **No Damp**® which has been specifically formulated to control a disease called damping off. **Cinnamon** powder is also an excellent deterrent for many fungi, so consider dusting the soil with this household condiment.

🍂 Many of the **seedlings** that you germinate at home **require bottom heat**. There are many specialized accoutrements available to accomplish this, such as germination mats. These "designer toys" for gardeners are little more than a heating pad for the seed trays, but they are effective. I have utilized the top of the refrigerator to provide bottom heat. It is always warm and holds two seedling flats quite nicely. Remember, temperatures over 80°F (26°C) can encourage diseases and poor plants.

🍂 **Air circulation is fundamental to the reduction of seedling fungal problems**. Too many times we feel that the developing plants "like" to be in the hazy humidity of a rainforest. This is partially true, but fresh air is crucial. Stagnant, humid air breeds endless amounts of mildew, molds, fungi and, as well, produces rather "watery and soft" growth. Choose germination compartments which have ventilators built into the clear covers or, during the day, lift the lids to allow in fresh air.

🍂 Developing **seedlings** will **require light**. If you prefer to use an artificial source, it should be moveable. The light source needs to be within a couple of inches (5 cm) of the tops of the seedlings. Often gardeners will place the lights out of range and the seedlings grow like "Jack's Beanstalk". Remember, transplanting into finishing containers usually takes place when the seedlings have two sets of true leaves. The initial leaf-like structures (cotyledons) are not considered as leaves.

CARROTS

Rippin' Roots and All

Spring is often the time of the year when a gardener's passive nature turns rather aggressive, at least when it comes to **increasing the perennial inventory**. **Root division** can be one of the most rewarding chores that occurs in the garden. Some plants that are divided in the spring are: Lysimachia, Pulmonaria or Lungworts, Siberian Iris, Peony, Daylily and Rhubarb.

One of the easiest methods of **dividing an old perennial**, is to use two garden forks. Once the plant is removed from the garden, stab the clump with the forks so that they are back to back. The curve of the tines will act as leverage to pry the plant apart. Most tough-rooted perennials will separate at a natural root lesion.

Root divisions make excellent legal tender for the gardener. We have all either been asked or have asked for a piece of this or that from a friend's garden. If you regularly divide your plants, you will always have something to trade. Transporting clumps is best done in moistened newsprint and a cardboard box lined with a garbage bag. I have successfully moved many a garden from province to province this way. If there is a great deal of top growth, you may experience damage, but the roots are generally fine.

Fall root division is often the suggested time in garden literature. This is sound advice if the gardener doesn't leave the transplanting too late in the season and autumn is usually a long season in your area. Prairie gardeners know that fall is often just a hiccup before hard frost and nasty weather set in for the winter. If you garden in a similar climate, divide and replant your perennials in August or very early September. Clay soil is also a determining factor on your timing for moving plants. These soils tend to expand when moistened and, if they are not suitably rooted in, the perennials will pop out of the soil at the first hard frost.

Dahlias and Cannas are popular plants for root division. As they both tend to grow an enormous number of roots, they should be divided each season. I like to do this prior to storage preparation so that I can take stock of what my crop has been like. Dahlias will divide at their weakest point; whereas Cannas take a fair bit of muscle to divide. Shake the soil off as best you can and look for obvious places to pull. If you must resort to using a sharp knife to divide the roots, dust the wounds with a powdered fungicide or Sulphur.

Graft and Corruption

🍃 Grafting two or more different varieties of plants together has long fascinated gardeners. Although not a particularly easy task for us, Mother Nature often supplies perfectly grafted specimens. When two branches or even roots of identical plants come in contact with each other, or perhaps crossed twigs on the same tree rub together, they often will intertwine and fuse together. I suppose it was these natural grafts that started plant enthusiasts wondering if they could do the same thing. One major rule in grafting is that the plants must be of the same family of plants or at least share familial similarities. One does not see oranges grafted onto Apple trees, yet.

🍃 **Hybrid Tea Roses** are most often budded onto tougher Rose rootstalk. Budding actually means that a single growth bud of the variety of Tea Rose is removed from the parent plant, inserted into a wound made on the wild rootstalk, and sealed over with either a latex band or a waterproof sealant. The bud will start to grow, obtaining sustenance from the established root of the other plant. Once the Rose grower is sufficiently sure that the bud has "taken", all remaining vestiges of the wild Rose are pruned away, leaving only the bud to take over. Upon examination of your Hybrid Tea Rose, you will see a large, knuckle-like portion at the base of the stems. This is the **bud union** site and, incidentally, the weakest portion of the Rose.

🍃 It is possible to actually have Roses of different colours and varieties budded onto a single root stalk, or several Apple varieties grafted onto a single tree. These oddities are often the "specials" in catalogue sales nurseries. However, there are many very practical examples of sensible unions. Grape varieties that are not strong enough to survive a frigid winter on their own roots are grafted to encourage vigour. **Apple varieties are grafted onto dwarfing rootstalk** so that they are more easily harvested, and more trees can be planted on less land.

🍃 If you wish to **attempt your own grafting,** I suggest that you invest some time in research at the public library or online. A picture is worth many words. Basically, the scion wood is the variety that is to be grafted and the rootstalk is the recipient. The term "cambium layer" will arise often in grafting discussions. This is the active growth area just under the bark. The success of your grafting attempts relies totally on your ability to match the cambium layers of both the scion and the rootstalk. The exceptions being incompatibility and certain viral infections.

One of the easiest grafts to do at home is between a *Zygocatus sp.*, **'Christmas Cactus'** and the recipient *Opuntia sp.* **'Bunny Ears'**. Here's what I have done to make a rather odd-looking Christmas tree. Remove the spines from the Opuntia Cactus, using a utility knife or sharp pruning knife. Slice into the edges of the Opuntia, making an incision the same length as a segment of the **Zygocactus**. If you space the incisions about the width of your finger apart, the resulting grafted cactus looks pretty full. Next, remove a single or double segment of the Zygocactus and carefully make a wedge shape of the cut end. Using the blade of your knife, pry open the incision on the Opuntia and insert the Zygocactus segment(s), aligning the wounded edges of both Cacti. Secure the segment(s) with a toothpick, ensuring that the wound is closed as tightly as possible. Once the edges are completely filled with segments, you can attempt a similar operation on the flat surface of the Opuntia. Within a few weeks, you will be able to tell which grafts took as they will be perky and starting to grow. Unsuccessful grafts will be wilted and can be removed. The plant will continue to grow Zygocactus segments and will eventually bloom. A real conversation piece.

Sexual Propagation

The term sexual propagation means developing new plants through seed. This differs from **asexual propagation** which deals with the reproduction of plants without the need of seed or spores. The term hybrid has come to mean more vigorous and, in many cases, better than the original. A hybrid cultivar is the offspring of two or more parents which are clones, or of pure inbred lines. This bit of genetic hoopla translates to mean that **seed from a hybrid plant doesn't always resemble the plant that it came from**. A pretty good trick for those who make their living from breeding specific forms of plants.

Seedling variation is actually a good thing for horticulture. Mother Nature provides us with plants that are not exactly like either parent or the rest of the family. Selections can be made from these oddball plants to improve the form, colour, blooming length, height and just about any genetic trait. Naturally forming mutants or **sports** are responsible for many of the variegated plants we have today, as well as for the wide selection of leaf forms and colours in plants like Hosta, for example.

❧ Producing specific seed or hybrid varieties can be accomplished in your own garden. Select the parents that you wish to cross-pollinate, ensuring that they bloom within relatively close time frames of each other. Select the seed-bearing plant and remove the male portion of the flower, leaving only the stigma. Secure a gauze netting around the flower so that unwanted insects bearing pollen can't get at the stigma. When the male portion of the other parent flower is ready, remove the pollen with a small paint brush and place it on the stigma of the seed-bearing plant. Cover the flower with the gauze. Once the ovary has swollen and ripened, you will be able to remove the seeds and start them in a nursery bed. The progeny will have some plants that resemble each of the parents and some which may have a blend of visible traits. There is no way for you to determine the genetic makeup of the seedlings, so trial and error and a lot of record keeping follow. It is fun, and developing a plant that is truly unique is rewarding.

❧ **Seed storage affects the germination of most varieties**. It is said, however, that seeds found in the ancient pyramids actually germinated several thousands of years after they were entombed. I recommend a more simplified approach to storage but cannot guarantee five thousand years of longevity. Seed is best stored in the refrigerator, in the vegetable crisper. My preferred containers are pill vials, or paper bags for larger seed. If you are storing left-over seed from a commercial source, keep it in the original packaging. Remember to always label seeds with the type and year that they were collected and placed in storage.

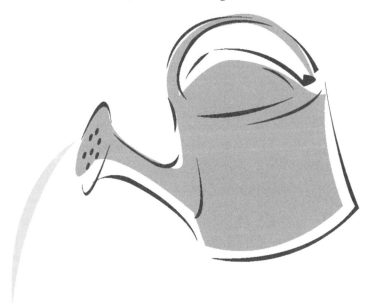

Garbage Gardening

The seeds or "pips" of Oranges and other citrus will germinate and produce great houseplants. It is unusual for these plants to produce flowers and fruit, but it does happen from time to time. Citrus prefer to have a rich, deep soil that is well draining. They all enjoy ample sunshine, and tend to be prone to spider mite infestations. **The Lemon seems to be the citrus that most often will produce fruit.** The citrus that we purchase is grafted onto selected rootstalks and most are hybrid varieties.

Papaya is a tropical fruit that is chock full of tiny black seeds. These seeds will germinate readily if they are treated properly. First off, the outer coating on each seed is called the aril. It feels like jelly and actually must provide the seed with some nutrient or protection in the wild. I like to dry the seed overnight on a paper towel, or rub the seeds on a paper towel to remove the aril. Plant the seeds in plantable peat pots as they do not transplant well. Grow them in a warm, moist environment to produce the largest specimens. **These plants often will flower indoors.**

Ginger roots make very reasonable plants for the classroom or the balcony landscape. As most Ginger is treated to prevent decomposition, look for a root at the green grocers which has already started to grow a bit. Plant the **Ginger root** into a very rich, humus soil, so that it is just below soil surface. Place the container in a bright sunny window and wait. The long, sword-shaped leaves will grow rapidly to produce a unique tropical-looking plant. I place my Gingers outdoors for the summer and move them back inside for the winter. They have yet to flower, but I do enjoy fresh Ginger root often.

Mango seeds are very large and somewhat unmanageable. They have a stringy outer shell that is covered with the slimy flesh of the Mango. Drying the seed is necessary just to be able to handle it easily. Often, the seed will have split open while still covered with the Mango, if this is so, the seed has already started to germinate. To increase the chances of this happening, **look for very overripe Mangos**. Place the seed with the largest end to the bottom of the pot. If you are unsure, lay the seed on its side in the pot, cover it with more soil, and it will eventually correct itself. The soil should be rich and composted and have the ability to hold lots of moisture. Once the seed is through the soil, place the plant in strong light and feed it with a high-Potassium soluble fertilizer.

Pumpkin seeds are a favourite snack food for many, but they also will keep well until the following season. When the jack-o'-lantern is being prepared, save the slimy seeds on newsprint. After a day or so they will have dried sufficiently to allow you to remove any vestiges of the Pumpkin pulp. The seeds can be stored in the refrigerator until early May, then sown to get a head start on your Pumpkin patch. I start them in peat pots so there is limited transplant shock. **Pumpkins enjoy rich soil** with a high content of manure or compost. They thrive in the sunlight and enjoy a variety of fertilizers to size their fruit.

Mama's 'lil Helpers – Rooting Hormones and Stimulants

There are products that can enhance the rooting process if they are used properly. **Over exuberance with a rooting hormone will cause the opposite effect to rooting.** When using a rooting powder, ensure that the proper strength is selected for the type of cutting you are rooting. Softwood or herbaceous cuttings, like Geraniums, require the first level or #1. Semi-hardwood cuttings like a Rose or Lilac may require #2, the next strongest hormone. The #3 grade is suggested for use on hardwood cuttings and dormant wood.

Rooting hormone is talc-like and generally coloured pink or blue, depending on the grade. Simply insert the wounded end of the cutting into the powder and then tap the cutting gently to remove any excess. **The cutting should appear to be slightly dusted,** not coated entirely. Insert the cutting into the rooting medium and wait for roots to develop.

There are other tricks to encourage cuttings to root without the use of auxins or synthetic products. One that I learned many years ago dealt with **the rooting of English Ivy**. Cuttings, or actually just long vines of Ivy, were gathered and rinsed with cool water. The strands were rolled up so they would fit into a heavy clear plastic bag. The plastic bag of Ivy was then placed into the cooler or refrigerated storage room. Within a few days, the Ivy had set roots at every leaf axil. The next step was to cut the Ivy into appropriate lengths, pot them and, presto, ready to go.

B U L B S

corms, rhizomes

*the root of
the problem*

Tulips and Other Heralds of Spring

🧅 Tulips, Daffodils and other spring-flowering bulbs should be fertilized as they decline. It is wise to use a feed that is high in Phosphorus such as 10-52-10 or bone meal. These fertilizers encourage strong root development and larger bulbs which translate to more flowers next season.

🧅 Dutch law states that **hybrid** Tulips cannot be exported until they are 4" (10 cm) in circumference, or bigger. Botanical or species Tulips are, by their nature, smaller than hybrid Tulips, therefore having smaller bulbs.

🧅 The tiny **Snowdrop,** or *Galanthus nivalis*, was named for the fair maid of February and in some countries is associated with Candlemas Day . . . February 2. In North America we celebrate that day awaiting the appearance of a large rodent and predict the climate based on whether or not he sees his shadow . . . hmmm?

🧅 **While seeds are dormant, bulbs are not.** They are living organisms which must be planted within a month or so from purchase time. Do not store them for planting next year as they will not produce very well.

🧅 Bulbs can be planted as soon as the soil at planting depth is below 61°F (16°C). Bulbs that are purchased early should be stored in a cool, dry place until planting time. **Do NOT store bulbs near ripening fruit**, in the refrigerator for example, as the ethylene gas that is given off will harm the bulbs.

🧅 Choose larger bulbs to accent a walkway or to plant around a lamppost or areas that will be seen up close. Consider smaller bulbs when you want to **create cost-effective mass plantings** which will be viewed from a distance.

🧅 Fall-planted bulbs require an extra boost of Phosphorus to encourage strong root development. Bone meal is generally incorporated into the base of the planting bed. Ensure that the fertilizer is mixed well with the base soil so as not to damage developing roots.

🧅 Gardens which provide a variation of colour and bloom size tend to be more interesting than monochromatic and mono-specific ones. Try planting a combination of Daffodils or Narcissus with a second layer of Tulips, followed by a top layer of Muscari. **This "layered" bulb garden can be containerized** in milder regions of the country.

Be adventuresome with colour for the spring garden. Nothing heralds this season quite like the golden and clear yellows of the Daffodil. Combine these horticultural workhorses with flamboyant Parrot Tulips and, perhaps, a mixture of delicate Grape Hyacinths to set them off. **Poor combinations are easily remedied the following year.**

Spring-flowering bulbs which have been forced indoors require good light after the flowers fade. **Remove the spent flowers and the stalks**, allowing the foliage to develop fully. Once outdoor bulbs are growing, plant the forced bulbs with them. They will flower the following year.

Tulips are so incredibly organized that it is possible to have a sequence of bloom from soon after the snow melts until June. Generally categorized by height and bloom time, these reliable spring-flowering bulbs carry names which honor special people. Examples are **Strauss**, **Chopin** and even **Pinocchio**.

Tulips which are about 6" (15 cm) tall belong to the **Gregii** and **Kaufmanniana** varieties. The latter has flowers characterized as Water Lily-shaped and they are quite large. The Gregii gang look lovely even after they have flowered as **their foliage has maroon markings on green**. These tend to be the earliest and shortest Tulips.

Single and double early Tulips are the second team of colour to show in the spring garden. Double Tulips resemble small Peonies or powder puffs of petals, and they stand sturdily against the early spring winds. Neither variety grows much taller than 18" (45 cm). **Apricot Beauty is my all-time favourite** in the single category, huge, peachy coloured with a fragrance that will waft for miles. **Monte Carlo** is the fragrant counterpart in the double early Tulips, it is bright spring yellow.

Tulip bulbs are rather fat and teardrop shaped. The larger end is the bottom of the bulb and the pointy end is the top. If you find this difficult to remember, just think that **Tulip bulbs are a lot like people.** Planting depth should be about two or three times the depth of the bulb, and plant in well-draining, rich soil. The distance apart depends on the type of show that is desired, but I plant them just so they are not touching each other.

A large expanse of bulbs is easily planted if you remove the soil down to the desired depth rather than plant each bulb individually. Place the bulbs in the pattern you want, firm them in, add a sprinkling of bone meal and cover them up. Watering is essential to establish a good root system, before heavy frosts render the bulbs dormant. The majority of root development takes place in the autumn that the bulbs are planted.

Once the Tulips and Daffodils have blossomed, there is a tendency for many gardeners to cut the leaves off and clean them up. This is the worst thing that you can do to the bulbs. The foliage is producing food for the bulb to size and ripen for the next season. **Cutting off the food supply is like signing a death warrant.** If the leaves are taking up more room than you anticipated, either lift the bulbs and replant them in an area where they can die down naturally, or work around the leaves.

Two Noses are Better Than One

Daffodils, which are in fact a Narcissus, have a bulb whose growing tips are called noses. When you are ordering Daffodils from a catalogue source, they should indicate if they are double or single nosed, this naturally affects the price. Older plants should have more noses and, therefore, more blooms.

The floral architecture of a Daffodil is rather interesting. The long snout-like apparatus is actually fused petals, known as the **trumpet or cup**. The six larger flat petals at the back are collectively called the **perianth**. Divisions of classification for Daffodils are based on the shape, structure and, in some cases, the size of these parts.

Large-trumpeted Daffodils are the best known of all the Narcissus classifications. These beauties are suited for naturalization or as specimen clumps in the spring flower bed. **Unsurpassable** and **Dutch Master** are both golden yellow, traditional daffs. **Mount Hood** is one of my personal favourites in this group, it is pure white.

- Split-cupped varieties of Daffodils look like they are wearing a coloured petticoat over the perianth. Often the cup is a contrasting colour and is somewhat ruffled. These oddities certainly do turn heads. One variety that is particularly striking, in my opinion, is **Palmares**. It has a clear white, almost creamy perianth with a solid peach pink crown. This variety will look lovely with **Apricot Beauty** tulips.

- Narcissus must have a deep well-draining soil, a rather light texture is also a benefit. Gardeners that have clay soil are advised to loosen the clay with ample amounts of composted steer manure, compost or even Peat Moss. With such amendments one would expect to grow great Narcissus year after year. Not so, the bulbs should be lifted every two to three years and the soil reworked.

- In zones USDA 2 and below, **Narcissus should be protected with a layer of mulch**. It is critical that the soil is well draining in these colder climates as the bulbs will not tolerate wet feet in the early spring. I have grown many varieties of Narcissus, with some effort, but planting them close to the house or where they are protected and get lots of snow cover seems to give the best results.

- Pink is not a colour associated with Daffodils, but it is very attractive nonetheless. **Rosy Cloud** is a variety that sports a Peony-like trumpet set against a stark white perianth. **Salome** and **Pink Pride** are great together, each supporting the subtle pink sunset tones of the other. **Salome** is a little shorter than the others, measuring in at about 18" (45 cm) and blooming in March or April.

- The petite, low-growing Daffodils are really charming. They clump and bloom just like the photos shown in the catalogues, without air brushing! I grow **Minnow**, a yellow and white baby that is very fragrant. **February Gold** stands sturdy to bear its diminutive flowers and clumps beautifully. **Sundial** is a flat, fragrant flower that resembles its namesake.

But Can I Eat Them Too?

🧅 **Allium** is the genus name for Onions but this is also a trade name for an ornamental classification of Onion relatives. The plants are, at best, bizarre with their globes of purple and white flowers resembling a basketball on top of a 3' (1 m) tall Onion stalk. Definitely a novelty for the gardener who has tried it all. Some call them **'Drumstick Onions'**, appropriately, I guess. They bloom later in the season and, apparently, can even keep some pests away.

🧅 *Allium giganteum*, the great granddad of all Onions, stands up to 4' (1.3 m) and has a huge purple floral head. The bulb is 7 to 8" (18-20 cm) in diameter, that's like a baseball. They often take a mid- to late-summer rest and start to develop roots in the autumn. They make their leaf growth in the winter, in mild climates, or in the spring for most of Canada. They flower at the end of their growing season, in spring or early summer.

🧅 Smaller Alliums abound on the market in colours ranging from yellow to burgundy. *Azureum* is a species that is a particularly good blue with *Moly* a strong yellow. These varieties have smaller, more manageable bulbs than their giant cousins.

🧅 Excellent drainage is the key to successfully blooming Alliums. I have small clumps of the yellow *Allium Moly* in my perennial border. The area is particularly sandy so the bulbs multiply well. Every few years, I dig them up and separate out the smaller bulbs. These Alliums are partnered with **Arctic Phlox** as a ground cover, so there is always a texture beneath the rather stark foliage.

Bearded Spring Wonders

🧅 **German Iris** are some of the easiest perennials to grow. They are distinguished from their kissing cousins the Siberian, Dutch and **Japanese Irises**, in that they have thick rhizomatous roots. A rhizome is like a swollen underground stem, similar to a fresh ginger root. The flowers also sport fuzzy segments on the falls or lower petals, hence the common name, Bearded Iris.

🧅 Bearded or German Iris come in a wide assortment of colours, and shades. This plant lacks red pigmentation gene, so maroons and oranges are the closest they get to that end of the spectrum. I am fond of the violets and the pinks. Try **Cranberry Crush** for a clear violet and **Panama Fling** or **Hidden World** for great pinks.

Hardiness is not much of a concern for Iris. They require a well-draining soil and lots of sun to flourish. I feed my Iris from time to time with bone meal and a soluble fertilizer high in Phosphorus. The rhizomes are planted so that about one-third is above soil level. They seem to enjoy the heat of the sun. Ideally, there should be five rhizomes per clump of Iris. **Note that they grow in one direction**, so if you plant the rhizomes with the growth facing outwards, your clump will eventually be bare in the centre. Try planting three facing outwards and two inwards. This way, the centre will always have foliage and flowers.

Wet Feet – Swamp Iris

Siberian Iris has a nice, hardy ring to it, doesn't it? Well, in general terms, if a plant has Siberian attached to it, hardiness is not a problem. The Iris is no exception. This tough trooper will grow in a wide range of soil and light conditions, but prefers to have wet feet. If you have a pond, this is a great plant to grow close to the edge so that its feet get wet from time to time. They bloom in May, are very strong rooted and considered to be heavy bloomers. Blue is the most common colour.

Water-loving Iris develop huge masses of roots. This makes the chore of dividing them rather difficult. Don't let the plants get overgrown or they will produce smaller flowers and make more work for you. After they have bloomed, using a sharp spade, slice the clumps into chunks about the size of your hand. This is a manageable size for me and renders a solid clump for the following season.

Dutch Iris

Dutch and Spanish Iris have bulbous roots, not rhizomes at all. These are the little gaffers that are on sale in the garden centres and department stores in colourful boxes and packets. Ranging in colours similar to the German Iris, these bulbs multiply quickly, giving a nice, massing effect. Rated for USDA Zone 4, they should have a winter mulch to ensure longevity in colder climates.

Bigger, Better Begonias

Tuberous Begonias are a classic for the shade garden or balcony containers. Classification for these behemoth bulbs is by floral description mostly and where they were developed. American and **Belgian Begonias are the most common**. Floral types include Camellia, which, as the name suggests, resemble the flat rosettes of the Camellia; **Fimbriata**, which resembles the flower of a Carnation, are somewhat ruffled; **Picotee**, which are two-toned, have one colour as a piping on the petal edges.

The largest of all Tuberous Begonias is one that I grew a few years back called **Estate Begonia**. Now, I was a tad skeptical when the catalogue description suggested that these tubers could produce upwards of 15 stems. Lo and behold, the tubers were the size of tea cup saucers and they did produce magnificently. The flowers were about 2" (5 cm) in diameter and there were hundreds of them, all in their vermillion to orange tones. The Estate Begonia tubers, as with the rest, can be divided as you would for planting Potatoes, by cutting the tuber into segments with "eyes" or growing buds. I divided these giants into pie sections and was very successful.

Emasculation is such a technical term, and a little intimidating at best. What is meant by this term is simply the removal of the male flowers. How do you tell the boys from the girls on a Begonia plant you may ask? The boys are the single flowers, with not a lot of embellishment, whereas the girls are the ruffled, fluffy or picotee that look like the picture on the container that they came in. Often there are two boys for each girl flower (not bad odds), one on each side of the female flower. Remove them as soon as you notice them to encourage a larger, fuller blossom.

Pendulous Begonias are delightful plants for a covered verandah or balcony that is in shade. The American hybrids tend to be the most popular of this strain as their flowers are plentiful and quite double. I like to start these tubers about three weeks earlier than my Begonias that are destined for pots. It is not that the pendulous Begonias take longer to sprout or grow, I just want them to be full and bushy when placed outside. Keep these hanging baskets free of strong winds, the foliage and stems are quite soft and will break easily.

Diets for Begonias actually start with the planting media. I use a well-composted manure, my own compost from the bin and Peat Moss as the base. It is difficult to describe the "feel" of the mix, but this is what determines when there is enough of one element or the other. Often, I will add Perlite® to improve the drainage. The ratio is roughly one-third of each with a couple of handfuls of moistened Perlite® per wheelbarrowful of mix.

Fertilizers from the realm of organic bases seem to be friendlier to the Begonia than most soluble types. Perhaps this is just my own experience, but I have ruined more plants with tender loving care and "too strong a mix" of fertilizer. **Remember that the roots of the Begonias are fibrous and very fragile.** Excess moisture, cool soil and even a hint of bacterial or fungal rot will ruin them in short order. I use fish fertilizers, seaweed blends, manure and compost tea, these being the easiest and least expensive alternatives. Often, fish-based fertilizers have a rather peculiar, strong and long-lasting bouquet.

Glads, Gladiolus, Gladioli

A corm is the description given for the "bulb-like" apparatus from which the popular Gladiolus develop. If you look closely, it really isn't a root at all, they appear on the bottom of the corm. The corm is actually a swollen, specialized portion of stem. One thing that is critical to the development of good corm size, and thus good flowers, is drainage. **Glads do not like to have their roots sitting in water.** When preparing the planting site, add a good layer of compost, Perlite®, sand or whatever material you prefer to ensure proper flow of water away from the corms.

Gladiolus gardeners have oodles of tricks for getting the best their plants can give. One such trick I have learned from Prairie gardeners is to **start the corms indoors**. The corms are started generally in flats of Peat Moss or a very high humus mix, bearing in mind that Glads must have good drainage. Start the corms in late April with bottom heat and, once sprouted, give them good light. The roots will mat in the flat, making transplanting fairly easy. If you start them too early, removal becomes detrimental, so start them in individual pots if planting earlier than April.

Gladiolus have a rather military abruptness to them. A tall, straight spike with no branches. From a design point of view, they need some softening to fit into the garden. **Try planting Glads with other perennials that have some height.** This way, the lush foliage of the companion plants will break up the stiff look of the Glad. Another good idea is to plant the Glads in succession so that they do not all bloom at the same time. **Space planting by a week or 10 days.** For goodness sake, please do not plant Glads in rows, they look even more like marching militia.

Bone meal is a favourite food for Gladiolus. Most bulbs, corms, tubers and rhizomes will react positively to a feed of higher Phosphorus. Bone meal works more slowly than soluble feeds, thus providing a constant dribble of Phosphorus over the growing season. High-Nitrogen feeds will produce enormous and very verdant plants, however, the blossoms seem to be the sacrifice made.

A florist trick to encourage the flowers of the Gladiolus to open more rapidly, and to have more flowers open per stem, is to pinch out the very top few inches of growth. The buds at the tip of the spike are very immature and, often, as Glads bloom from the bottom of the spike upwards, will never amount to much. This holds true for cut Glads in the house, too.

Thrips are very common on Gladiolus, unfortunately. These critters are very small and can ravage the flowers in short order. There are many chemicals which are sold to control thrips, but water alone can be useful. Thrips pupate in the top few centimeters of the soil. Frequent flooding of the area around the plants will drown the developing insects. Also, overhead watering will reduce the number of adults in and around the plants.

Storage of Gladiolus corms is necessary as they will not tolerate winter in the ground. After flowering, the Glads should be left to manufacturing food for the developing corm(s). It is now that higher Phosphorus feeds are beneficial. As the leaves start to yellow, this indicates that the plants should be lifted and stored. I remove all but a short handle of top growth and leave it attached to the corm. **They dry outside much the same as you would dry Onions to ripen them.** It is wise to dust the corms with all-purpose insecticide/fungicide prior to final storage. Place the corms in a paper bag, add the product and shake. This coats the corm and readies them for dry storage. Keep the storage area dry, cool and dark. The handles of foliage that you left on will now separate easily from the corms.

Gigantic Blooms With Limited Work

Amaryllis, ah yes, we all have had at least one of these giants in our gardening career. Recently, **Amaryllis have become very popular.** This fame is most likely attributed to the vast amount of breeding work that has been going on in the latter part of the last century. It used to be that red or white with a few pink tones in between were all that one could grow. Today, there are doubles, multi-flowering stems, scented and miniatures to choose from. Colours range from soft apricot, rich mahogany through the deliberate reds to soft pastel pinks and, of course, pure white.

Amaryllis are of African origin and therefore require a dry dormant period at some part in their life cycle. Customarily, these bulbs are available on the retail market for the winter holiday season, arriving in conjunction with the spring-blooming Tulips and Daffodils. A good bulb will have a firm texture when you apply pressure with your fingers. Look for a specimen that has no scars, mold or other unusual disfigurements. The roots will be dried out and, in some cases, not there at all. Damaged, fleshy-rooted specimens should be avoided.

Requirements for growing an Amaryllis are very few. The pot needs to be only slightly larger than the bulb itself. I like to be able to just place a finger between the sides of the container and the bulb. The planting mixture should be high in Peat Moss or other compost-like material. Drainage is very important. The bulb is planted with one-third of it showing on top of the planting mix. One good watering is sufficient until the planting mix is dry to the touch. Often, the flower stalk appears before the leaves. Fertilizer is not recommended at this stage.

Once Amaryllis bulbs have bloomed, they seem to cause a certain amount of concern as to their care. I have grown them for years with varying degrees of success, but they are always worth the minimal effort they require. Continue to grow the plant in the best light that you can give it. Normally, there are huge, strap-like leaves in need of support and nothing else. Once the danger of frost has passed, plant the bulb outdoors, in a manner similar to what you did in the container. **If you have grown Onions, Amaryllis require similar conditions.** Good sun, drainage and moderate Phosphorus feeds. In September, or before frost, lift the bulbs, pot them and bring them indoors. Gradually reduce the water so as to cause the leaves to yellow. This ripening period will take about three weeks to a month. Once yellowed, put the whole works away in a dry, warm, dark location for eight weeks. Bring the bulbs out of storage about eight weeks prior to when you want them to bloom. **There are no guarantees** that the plants will rebloom, but often they will.

Aphrodite is a variety of Amaryllis which is considered double. It is truly a spectacular plant, offering the signature-size flowers of the species with twice the number of petals. The range of tone is predominantly pink or blush on a white background. As a compliment to **Aphrodite's** beauty, **Blossom Peacock** has a fragrant double flower. This variety sports darker pink to red edges on a clear white background. Both plants are as easily grown as the original species.

Amaryllis can also be grown in a glass, similar to Hyacinths. This process of growing and displaying a bulb requires close attention and certain precautions. Plants which are rooted in water produce a different type of root than those in soil or a similar media. Keeping the roots healthy in water demands that the water be changed periodically. The glasses available for Hyacinths will not support their humongous cousins, the Amaryllis, so look for glasses specially designed for them. Put a layer of horticultural-grade charcoal in the glass to ensure that the water stays clean. Place the bulb in the top and watch what happens. This is a very artistic way to display an Amaryllis. Remember, **Amaryllis also make great cut flowers**.

Morticia Adams Loved Calla Lilies

Calla Lilies are popular container plants for most of North America. Recently, as pond popularity has grown, interest in callas has increased. **Callas enjoy moist conditions** and will flourish if their roots are soaked periodically, making them ideal candidates for the edge of a pond or stream. These South African natives are hardy in USDA zones 9-11, and they also make great houseplants. If you grow Callas indoors, they like a soil mix that is very rich in humus. Moisture is imperative and good light conditions preferred. I have grown them in a greenhouse situation under the shade of palms and less dense foliage plants. They thrive all winter long with a minimum of attention.

Calla varieties are becoming quite exciting. The species is white but, today, the range is from the deep golden yellows of *C. Ellotianna* to flame reds and soft pastel pinks and purples. Some Callas will have spotted or freckled foliage, which is an added bonus.

Storage of Calla bulbs can be confusing for some. If you decide not to grow the plants all season long, store them in moist Peat Moss or sphagnum. Moist means that you can wring the moss in your hand and a small amount of water will drip out. Any more and the mix is too wet, any less and the bulbs will dry out.

To encourage strong stems on the somewhat "watery" growth of the Calla Lily, I encourage the use of **higher-Potassium soluble fertilizers. 10-10-27** is sold under the name Phostrogen®. I have often wondered why the name supports Phosphorus when actually the Potash has the higher percentage. Maybe "Potashtrogen" sounded like it should be used in a hormone replacement therapy rather than plant food!

Containerized Calla Lilies often produce better if they are not over potted. There is wisdom in keeping plants in smaller containers, for many reasons. One is simply for room. Over potted plants will tend to spend a great deal of time producing roots to fill the pot, at the expense of the flowers.

⚬ ***Colocasia esculenta*** are great partners for Calla Lilies. These **Elephant Ears**, as they are often known, prefer a rich moist soil too. This plant comes from the South Pacific Islands, I'm confident that I have eaten it as **Taro**. Growing to about 5' (1.5 m) tall in North America, this lush, heavy-leaved plant imparts a tropical splendor to any garden. The bulbs are kept in cool, moist storage for the winter, unless you garden in USDA zones 9 or higher.

⚬ **Caladiums** resemble their larger cousins, Elephant Ears, but are more colourful, with smaller leaves. Their foliage looks artificial to me as it is so brightly coloured and in rather odd combinations. Pink with green and clear segments that resemble plastic. Spots, freckles, crinkles, ruffles and truly weird flowers make these container or bedding plants the talk of the neighbour hood. The bulbs are lifted for the winter months and stored in their pots, dry and warm. They sleep for about eight weeks then off they go again in a flourish of colour and truly tropical splendor. If you have a pond in the garden, place the Caladiums in terra cotta pots and set them on the water's edge. This way, they will get a regular soaking and love it.

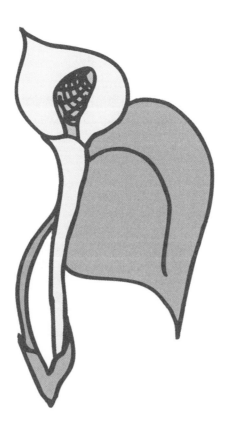

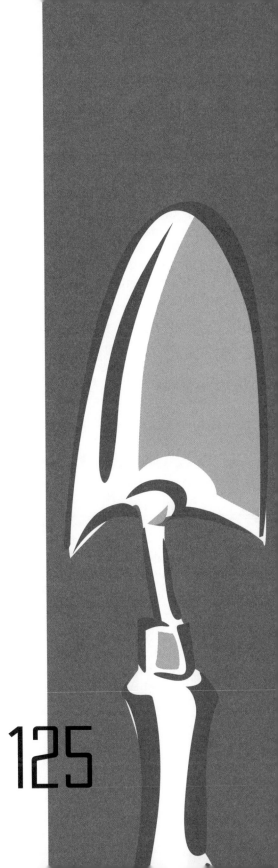

MAINTENANCE

how to

&

pruning

125

A Good Gardener Never Blames the Tools!

Garden tools will remain in better shape longer if you perform a few simple tasks. **Never put tools away dirty!** They should be cleaned and coated with a light coating of cooking oil to prevent rusting. Always use a shovel or a spade that has been sharpened . . . it seems to makes the job easier.

It is a good idea to have more than one lawn mower blade on hand. Once the active blade on the machine has dulled, remove it and replace it with your spare "sharpened" blade. **Rotate the blades on a regular basis** to ensure that the turf is being cut as opposed to being ripped by the blade.

Wooden-handled garden tools have long been the standard. Blisters, for most gardeners, are also a standard. To avoid or at least reduce the number of blisters, try applying a coating of wax to the wooden handles of shovels, hoes or other heavily used tools. Floor wax seems to last longer than anything else.

Where do I Plant this One?

Rhubarb provides a marvelous "textural" element to any perennial garden, as well as to the vegetable patch. In spring, Rhubarb enjoys a heavy feed of well-rotted manure or **manure tea**. To make the tea, soak a burlap sack of old manure in a large barrel or pail. Let it stand for at least a week. The resulting solution is powerful. The strength of the solution increases in ratio to the length of soaking time.

Taller plants will require support of some sort during the growing season. Metal rings, hoops and stakes are often used, however, **prunings from deciduous trees make a more "natural" stake** which is easily camouflaged. Several twigs intertwined with the plant will provide effective support.

The Kindest Cuts of All

Lilacs herald spring with magnificent splendor. Once the blossoms are spent, it is a good idea to remove the brown flower heads. This "tidying" not only improves the look of the shrub, but allows you an opportunity to check for insects. **Do not prune Lilacs in June**, fresh wounds tend to encourage Lilac borers.

Hedges which are trimmed with shears or electric clippers generally appear crisp and highly manicured. Eventually, hedges maintained in this manner will require "reworking" to rejuvenate the structure of the hedge. Secateurs or loppers are best used for this task.

Raspberries and other caned fruit should be pruned in the early autumn. Remove this year's fruiting canes to the ground and reduce the new growth to approximately chest height. A liberal application of high Phosphorus will encourage strong root growth and sturdy canes for next year's crop.

Forsythia shrubs should not be pruned in the fall, if at all possible. The flower buds are forming for the following year's show at this time of the year. They are **best pruned after flowering** to maintain height and strong blooming habit.

Apple trees should be pruned during their dormant period. In some parts of Canada, late February is the starter pistol for this often tedious chore. Remove and dispose of the pruned branches to avoid fungal reinfection, and spray the trees with dormant oil and lime Sulphur.

Bougainvillea should be cut back severely in the autumn in order to produce abundant colourful bracts indoors. These somewhat scrambling vines can be reduced by 75% without harm. Grown in very strong light, and fertilized with a balanced feed, colour appears well before it would be possible to enjoy them outdoors.

Grapes are a super plant for providing privacy, even if they are pruned properly. **The tendency for most North American gardeners is to prune Grapes too lightly.** Traditionally, vines are reduced to six or seven healthy stems with the same number of buds. This may seem drastic, but the new growth will push faster and produce more flowers and fruit. Pruning is generally done in late February or early March, depending on the season, but always when the plants are dormant. The debris should be removed and discarded or burned to prevent any fungal reinfection.

Beautiful White Birch have suffered terribly over the past several years on the Prairies. Although Birch is common in northern Alberta, Saskatchewan and Manitoba, in the southern clay belt they struggle. A condition known as **"Birch die back"** has all but eliminated White Birch from residential landscapes. In more favorable areas of the country, Birch are pruned in the early summer. Dormant pruning is not advised as this species will "bleed" so much that the tree is stressed for the season. Also, **the scent of sap encourages Bronze Birch Borer and Leaf Miner to attack.**

American Elms, or at least what is left of them, should not be pruned past mid-June. In some areas of North America, wise administrators and governments have enacted legislation to control pruning. The trees are so susceptible to the Elm Bark Beetle that running sap and open wounds invite in these predaceous bugs. These beetles are the vectors for **Dutch Elm Disease** so any control measures should be heeded.

Suckers on Lilacs, Chokecherry and many of the grafted horticultural varieties of trees keep the gardener in good exercise, in removing them. **Do not be tempted to prune the "suckers" out.** This actually encourages more growth, as does top pruning. The most reliable way to remove suckers, is to pull them for as long as you physically can, then cut the roots below soil level. Spraying the suckers with a non-selective herbicide is not a great idea, these products translocate or move throughout the plant's system, and you could damage the parent tree.

Food For Thought

Garden Chrysanthemums require a good feed in the early autumn as most varieties set buds as the days start to get shorter. Varieties developed at Morden, Manitoba, however, set buds as a result of high heat. No matter what variety you grow, a good fertilizer to use is 18-18-21, or any Tomato food.

Seaweed fertilizer combined with 10-52-17 is a rather unusual combination, but extremely effective. One grower blends this concoction with a soil-wetting agent or surfactant. His results are astonishing. If you are looking for a brand name, try "Grower's Eagle" for the **10-52-17** and Organican® **2-5-2** for the seaweed. Both are available in Winnipeg, Canada at Grower's Fertilizer Limited.

Time-releasing fertilizer is the way to go for hanging baskets, planters or large commercial installations. One popular brand is Osmocote® 14-14-14. The product resembles small, beige peas which pop between the fingers if enough pressure is exerted. The concept here is that the **Osmocote®** is incorporated into the planting mix prior to installation of plants. When the baskets or containers are watered a small amount of available nutrient is released. In most cases, one application is sufficient for the entire growing season. Examine a commercial nursery planting mix the next time that you buy a plant. You will probably notice these little fertilizer spheres.

Healthy, Heavy Harvests

 Raspberries and **Blackberries** will not spoil as quickly if they are picked in the morning. Raspberries should be picked when the fruit is just starting to leave the stem. Blackberries are harvested when they become sweet, not necessarily when they first turn black. Both should be kept in cool storage.

 Strawberries perform well when mulched with either an organic or inorganic mulch. Well-rotted steer manure worked into the soil will provide enough nutrients to keep the plants in production all season. Runners can be separated from the parent plants to form new colonies once the primary harvest is completed.

 Cabbage plants can follow a planting of early harvested peas. Peas and Beans will fix Nitrogen in the soil and the Cabbages will benefit. **Fall Cabbage** will last longer in the sun than its spring cousins, which must be harvested as soon as the heads mature.

 Carrots may be planted in late summer so that you can enjoy a snack of fresh fall veggies. Caution should be taken to increase the amount of water as the plants emerge. I like to soak the row before the seed is planted, then once again after the seed is covered. **Mulching works wonders for summer seedlings.**

Weed Wars

Sow Thistle, Goatsbeard and many other garden weeds will have full seed heads in late August. To ensure a cleaner garden next season, remove as many of the weeds as is possible and watch for their seedlings in September. Spray or remove these plants as they can overwinter.

The most effective time of the year to eradicated deeply rooted **perennial weeds** is the autumn. If you think about it, these hardy souls are pumping nutrients down into their tap roots so that they can withstand the rigors of a frosty winter. Applications of either **2,4-D®** products or **Glphosinates** like **RoundUp® Wipe Out®** or **Erase®** will have them gone before the snow flies.

Chickweed is only good in a salad! In the garden, this feisty wee weed reigns supreme. A verdant crop of this scourge indicates that the soil it is growing in is very high in Nitrogen and is usually damp. It seeds (already germinated seeds I think) profusely, some of which will even grow on top of the mulch. **Many have tried but few have conquered the omnipresent Chickweed.** The only saving grace is that it is green. Could you imagine the embarrassment if it was bright blue or red? Everyone would know that I have the largest collection of Chickweed in the country. Pulling it out by hand seems to be the only safe way to reduce the population.

Weeds come to the garden from a number of sources. One such source is barnyard manures. If the gardener is a little hasty, and gleans the topmost portion from the manure pile, the weed population will be astonishing. Take some time and dig into the oldest pile of manure, it is there that gardener's gold is found.

Of Pots and Pans

Shrubs and perennials are often relocated in the fall. Containerized plants from the nurseries and garden centres are generally reduced in price, making them difficult to resist. **Remember to prepare the planting area well**, add composted manure or other organic matter, a transplant fertilizer or bone meal and lots of water. A layer of mulch is often a good idea.

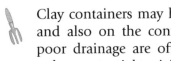

Clay containers may have a white crust which forms on the soil and also on the container's surface. Excessive fertilization and poor drainage are often the cause of this "salts" build up. To reduce potential toxicity, improve the drainage and water liberally to flush out the salts.

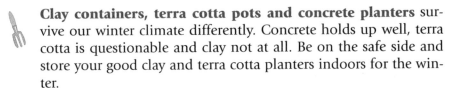

Clay containers, terra cotta pots and concrete planters survive our winter climate differently. Concrete holds up well, terra cotta is questionable and clay not at all. Be on the safe side and store your good clay and terra cotta planters indoors for the winter.

Recycling containers from year to year is an excellent habit to get into, but so is cleanliness. Plastic planters, window boxes, tubs and even terra cotta containers should be squeaky clean prior to planting your new crop. I like to use a solution that contains a couple of "glugs" of household bleach in 2 gallons (8 L) of water. This solutions should be used as the second to final rinse of the containers. Clear water as the final flush is advised.

Don't Forget!

Irrigation lines should be prepared for the winter at the first signs of frost. If you have not had the lines "blown" with compressed air, or if you're a bit worried at the unpredictable weather, turn the supply lines off and leave the valves half open.

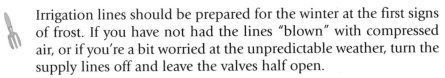

Roses, cut fresh from the garden, are delightful in floral arrangements. To extend the life of cut Roses, **take a container of water to the garden** and plunge the freshly cut stems into the water immediately. Recut the stems under water prior to arranging.

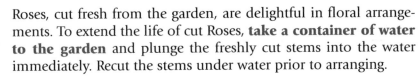

Seed catalogues start arriving in very early spring or even before Christmas. Take a few precautions before you make that order . . .. Remember the size of your growing space, the amount of actual time that you have to dedicate and . . . your budget.

Datura flowers are exquisitely scented and at their peak in the evening. Position your container so that you can benefit from this exotic scent as you relax on the patio. Varieties that are readily available are:

Datura **"Double Golden Queen"** (5'/1.5 m)
Datura **"La Fleur Lilac"** (18"/45 cm)
Datura **"Meteloides"** (5'/1.5 m)
Datura **"Sauveolens"** (10'/3 m)
Seeds are available from Thompson and Morgan
P.O. Box 1308 Jackson, NJ 08527-0308 or phone 1-800-274-7333

December is the time of the year to zealously mark all of the **"new" items that you are going to "need"** for next season. Place the catalogue in a spot where it can be referred to often during the day. Make a wish list of new seeds and plants for others to "share". We are approaching a season of gift giving, after all.

Shrubs and trees festively festooned for the winter season with lights are in little danger of damage. The heat produced from outdoor lights may cause some foliar drying, but the winter sun causes much more damage.

Warm, moist soil decreases transplant shock and encourages strong root development. Prior to planting Tomato transplants, moisten the soil with warm water and a high Phosphorus fertilizer in solution. Cover the planting area with black plastic for several days. At planting time, remove the plastic to reveal a toasty warm planting bed for your Tomatoes.

Battling Bugs

Purchase Dormant Oil and Lime Sulphur in preparation for spraying when the temperatures maintain above zero consistently. The battle against **Rhizosphera Needle Cast** (brown spruce, cedar and pine) begins as soon as the temperatures remain above zero. Remember that **Colorado Blue Spruce must NOT be sprayed with Dormant Oil**, substitute insecticidal soap or a surfactant.

Earthworms in the garden are, or should be, welcomed guests. If worm castings are unsightly to you or the soil appears to be less porous, **do not blame the worms**, simply add more organic matter.

A seasoned gardener from the Richmond Garden Club in British Columbia, Canada, shared his aphid spray with me. I have not yet tried his elixir but he swears by it. Combine ½ cup (125 mL) of rubbing alcohol (isopropyl) with 1 tsp. (5 mL) of Tabasco® sauce, and 2 oz. (60 mL) Murphy's Oil Soap®. The mixture is agitated lightly then aimed at the aphids . . . try it, and thanks to Grant Williams.

Timing is everything when it comes to insect control. Try to learn the life cycle or habits of the culprit bugs before you attempt to control them. Seasonal applications of control measures work best when they can kill more than one life stage of the insect.

Vines and Twines

Clematis in her various shades and forms, is the cause of many pruning questions. In harsh climates, there are only a handful of Clematis which will survive above the snow line. The remaining, predominantly hybrid, varieties can be cut back in the fall. I have found that even with the hardiest varieties, their stems are so brittle that any manipulation tends to break them off. The easiest variety to prune is *C. macropetala* **'Blue Bird'** and *C.m.* **'Markham's Pink'**.

Dropmore Honeysuckle is a very hardy vine. It does require pruning to keep it in check and in good blooming habit. I prune the weaker growth and stems which are traveling in the wrong direction in the early spring. This way, I have a chance to see the extent of the winter damage. A late summer pruning can also be beneficial in zones 5 and up. Colder areas of the country may stand to lose any new growth that may be stimulated as a result of the pruning.

Hops or *Humulus lupus*, are one of the fastest growing vines in North America. **A severe pruning is often the prescription for these rampant growers**, simply to keep them within boundaries. They will die back in zone 2, but in most other regions they may bud out from the older wood. The prunings are contorted and rather artistic, in a sense. They can be very useful in floral arrangements and crafts.

Old Age is a Good Thing

Mock Orange shrubs, or *Philadelphus coronarius* in the trade, are beauties for the right garden. However, inappropriate pruning can throw the blooming schedule out the window. Either just after flowering or in the early spring, Mock Oranges should have about one-third of their older wood removed. These shrubs form flowers on mature wood so it is important to always have some new wood that is maturing.

Weigela is a pleasant shrub to have in the garden and it is touted as being somewhat insect and disease free. The best plants are pruned annually after the flowers fade to remove some of the older wood. This practice is encouraged to keep the plants to a reasonable size. Leave a selection of different ages of wood so there will always be blooming-age wood.

Spirea varieties offer a wide range of colours and sizes, from golden-leafed specimens to flame red. The flowers on the old farmstead species **S. X vanhouttei** are perhaps the most spectacular. **Bridal Wreath Spirea**, as it is known to many, requires pruning to keep it in check. Older wood once again is the blooming wood. So a judicious trim once the flowers are past is usually enough to keep the flowers coming for the following season. Reworking or downsizing a mature shrub often jeopardizes the season's bloom.

Evergreen – Ever Pruned

Junipers require regular tidying to look their best. Lift the branches that are to be trimmed and locate a secondary branch that is growing in a similar direction to the one you wish to remove. It is at this junction that you make your cut. The secondary growth will fall into place, pointing in the same direction that the removed piece did. This does not destroy the shape of the plant and the foliage will cover the white wound. Please **avoid using hedge shears to prune Junipers**, unless you are shaping a topiary.

Spruce, Pine and most conifers are kept in shape through a pruning process called **"candling"**. If you look at the growing tips of a conifer, you will see that the new growth is a soft, pliable candle-like structure. Removal of this terminal growth causes latent lateral buds to break and form a bushier looking plant. **Mugho Pine** is one of the most commonly candled plants.

Skirting or removing the lower branches of evergreens is a common practice, unfortunately. If the trees are planted too close to a driveway or walkway, people trim the lower branches for access. Others simply remove the lower branches so they can cut the lawn under the tree. If you look at any conifer in its natural habitat, the skirt flows out over the ground providing a natural defense from competitive plants. **Turf does very poorly under conifers** anyway, so leave the skirt alone.

Cedar or **Arborvitae**, will have many brown inner branches. The fans of foliage eventually block off enough light that the inner branches cannot function. The foliage dies and leaves a brown, crisp patch. If you remove the foliage from this area, or because of reworking the shrub, expose the brown to the sunlight, often the branches resprout. The browning is natural and is often improperly diagnosed as winter kill or a mite infestation, it is simply lack of light.

Pruning Flowers – is this a good thing?

Snapdragons will perform at their very best if they are pinched at transplant time. The singular stalks will produce, yes you've got it, a singular flower, if left alone. A single pinching stimulates side shoots to develop, each of which will bloom.

Petunias grow in a rosette form, spreading out from a central stem. If you pinch the side shoots after flowering, they will develop even more blooming stalks. The term **"dead heading"** is often associated with Petunias. This is just the term given to the removal of spent flowers and a light pruning.

Roses should be pruned each time you take a Rose blossom off. Too often we just cut the floral stem and leave the cane to hopefully produce more. I try to remove the cane down to the first true leaves (a five leaflet arrangement) when I remove a blossom. My Roses have a short growing season so if I cut back any further, they often will not produce any more flowers on that stalk.

An Ounce of Prevention is Worth . . .

Pruning equipment should be kept clean, sharpened and disinfected as a matter of habit. Secateurs or hand shears dull over time, use a whet stone to sharpen the curved cutting blade. There are jigs available to secure the blades for sharpening, but a good stone used regularly will suffice. **Gasline anti-freeze is an excellent disinfectant** for shears, loppers and saws. Alcohol and bleach will also work but they tend to rust the equipment. Always disinfect your tools between cuts if you suspect a blight or fungal problem.

The results of your pruning will show in a few seasons if you have not done a good job. When removing a branch, always attempt to **make the cut as flush to the collar as possible**. The collar is easily determined as it looks like the bark is wrinkled where the limb is attached to the main trunk. Removal of the collar will lengthen the healing time.

Covering a pruning wound at one time was the accepted practice. The products ranged from an asphalt-based black paint to latex. Research over the years has proven that painting a wound only encourages decay and actually slows down the healing process.

Ragged wounds and scars that have resulted from weather damage need to be cleaned before they will heal properly. Remove the rough edges around the wound with a very sharp utility or pruning knife. I trace the outline to resemble a boat with pointed bow and stern. **The cleaner the edges of the wound the faster the cambium layer will heal.**

Stump removal is the final stage of a big job. Poplar trees seem to require adequate stumping before they cease sending up suckers from the dying roots. Commercial equipment and crews are available to grind the stump away well below the soil line. In the event that the equipment cannot access your garden, **an old-fashioned stump remover will work**. Drill holes into the stump at about 2" (5 cm) intervals. Mix 10 parts diesel fuel to 1 part 2,4-D® and pour it into the holes. The stump will decompose over a couple of years.

Index

A

Acidic soil – 44, 47
Aechmea fasciata – 50, 93
Aeration – 20, 24
African Violets – 63, 94, 98
Agave – 88
Alkaline soil – 8, 27, 37, 39, 44, 47, 67, 70, 78, 79
Allium Moly – 116
Allium – 116
Aloe barbadensis – 89
Aloe Vera – 89
Amaryllis – 92, 121, 122
Ammonium nitrate – 18
Angel's Trumpet – 85
Anti-transpirant – 56
Ants – 13, 24, 77
Aphids – 34, 63, 72, 73, 76, 82, 133
Apple scab – 72
Apples – 57, 60, 61, 72, 91, 93, 106, 127
Apricot trees – 60, 113, 115, 121
Aquilegia – 59, 96
Arugula – 39
Azaleas – 44, 92

B

Baking soda – 55
Basil – 30, 31, 33, 57, 86
Basil, Blue African – 30, 33
Basil, Siam Queen – 33
Basil, Spicy Globe – 86
Bean, Castor Oil – 96
Beans, Pole – 70
Beans, Scarlet Runner – 12
Beetles, cucumber 77
Beets – 42, 70
Begonias – 94, 97, 118, 119
Begonias, Belgian – 118
Begonias, Estate – 118
Begonias, Pendulous – 118
Begonias, Picotee – 118
Begonias, Tuberous – 118
Biennials – 97
Birch – 128
Birch die back – 128
Birds – 26
Black knot – 55
Black-Eyed Susan – 16,
Blackberries – 129
Black flies – 54

Blades, lawnmower – 18, 20, 21, 26, 126
Blood meal – 68, 78
Blossom-end rot – 61
Blueberries – 44
Bone meal – 8, 13, 42, 44, 78, 79, 89, 112, 114, 117, 120
Bordeaux mixture – 60
Boston Ferns – 84
Bougainvillea – 127
Broccoli – 70
Brugmansia – 85, 97
Brunnera – 10
Brussels sprouts – 70
Bryophyllum – 98
BTK® – 58
Bugs, mealy – 54, 64
Bulbils – 102
Bulbs – 28, 33, 34, 58, 90, 92, 102, 103, 104, 112-124
Burlap – 26, 126
Butterfly, cabbage – 54, 61, 71

C

Cabbage butterfly – 54, 61, 71
Cabbage worms – 58
Cabbage – 32, 39, 48, 54, 58, 61, 70, 71, 129
Cabbage, Fall – 129
Cacti – 51, 88, 89, 107
Cacti, spines – 88, 107
Cacti, True – 51, 88
Cactus, Christmas – 88, 107
Cactus, Saguaro – 89
Caladiums – 124
Calceolaria – 83
Calcium deficiency – 61
Cambium – 106, 136
Camomile – 32
Candling – 135
Canes, Raspberry – 78, 127
Cankerworms – 57
Canna Lily – 9, 105
Cantaloupe – 42, 79
Caper spurge – 59
Capsaicin – 76
Carbon – 42, 43
Carrots – 33, 40, 70, 73, 76, 129
Cats – 28, 48, 59
Cauliflower – 70

Cedar – 46, 132, 135
Cherry – 55
Chickweed – 130
Chicory – 74
Chinch bugs – 24
Chives – 72, 73
Chokecherry – 55, 57, 101, 128
Chrysanthemums – 15, 40, 93, 128
Cineraria – 83
Cinnamon – 103
Citronella – 56, 57
Citrus mitis – 94
Citrus – 94, 109
Clay soil – 20, 26, 44, 45, 46, 48, 49, 51, 76, 105, 115, 128
Clematis – 44, 133
Clivia miniata – 91
Cloche – 36, 70, 71, 79
Cobaea scandens – 54
Coconut fibre – 86
Coffea arabica – 89
Coffee – 43, 89
Coleus – 96
Collar – 62, 136
Columbine – 59, 96
Companion Plants – 8, 11, 32, 33, 69, 73, 120
Compost tea – 43, 119
Compost – 12, 34, 42, 43, 44, 46, 48, 51, 61, 62, 63, 66, 67, 68, 71, 73, 74, 75, 77, 78, 79, 82, 86, 109, 110
Conifers – 135
Coral bells – 8
Coriander – 33
Cormels – 103
Corms – 103, 119, 120
Corn – 68, 69
Crab grass – 22
Crabapple trees – 60, 72
Crassula – 98
Creeping Charlie – 23
Cross-pollination – 69
Cucumber beetles – 77
Cucumbers – 77
Cut, flush – 100, 101
Cutting, root – 101
Cuttings – 37, 75, 85, 96, 97, 98, 99, 100, 101, 103 110, 136
Cutworms – 62, 69

D

Daffodils – 112, 114, 115, 121
Dahlias – 60, 103, 105
Dandelion – 22, 72
Datura – 85, 96, 97, 132
Davallia fijiensis – 86, 100
Daylilies – 16, 105
Dead heading – 135
Deer-resistant plants – 59
Delphiniums – 15, 54
Dieffenbachia – 93, 99
Digitalis – 59, 97
Dill – 34
Dipel® – 58
Disease, black knot – 55
Disinfectant – 136
Dividing – 9, 11, 40, 75, 105, 117, 118
Docking – 100
Dog spots – 24
Dolichos lablab – 84
Dormant Oil – 60, 63, 127, 132
Double dig – 45
Drainage – 16, 25, 26, 28, 46, 50, 86, 101, 116, 119, 121, 122, 131

E

Earthworms – 24, 40, 132
Earwigs – 60
Easter Lily – 83
Edging – 20, 22, 24, 45
Elephant Ears – 124
Elms, American – 57, 128
Elms, Dutch Elm Disease – 128
Emasculation – 118
Endive – 74
Endive, Belgian – 74
Epimedium – 11
Epiphyllum – 88
Epiphytic plants – 50, 87
Epsom salts – 66, 91
Escarole – 74
Ethylene – 93, 112
Evening Primrose – 14

F

False Indigo – 59
Fennel – 33, 34
Fennel, Florence – 34
Ferns – 84, 86, 100
Ferns, Boston – 84
Ferns, Maidenhair – 12
Ferns, Ostrich – 12
Ferns, Rabbit's Foot – 86, 100

Fertilizer – 21, 22, 42-44, 128, 129
Fertilizer, high-Phosphorus – 21, 22
Fertilizer, time-releasing – 129
Fescue – 21, 27
Feverfew – 40
Flame of the Woods – 82
Flea beetles – 61
Forsythia – 127
Foxgloves – 97
Fritillaria – 58
Fungi – 55, 103, 104
Fungicide – 9, 19, 31, 55, 96, 97, 102, 103, 105, 120
Fungicides, broad-spectrum – 55
Fungus gnats – 54

G

Garlic – 73, 86
Geranium, Cranesbill – 72
Geraniums – 72, 99, 110
Germination – 21, 26, 28, 39, 45, 60, 66, 73, 76, 77, 79, 85, 96, 97, 104, 108, 109, 130
Ginger – 109
Gladiolus – 63, 103, 119, 120
Globe Thistle – 15
Gloxinia – 94
Glphosinates – 130
Golden Glow – 15
Gooseberries – 55
Gourds – 80
Grafting – 101, 106, 107, 109, 128
Grapes – 32, 106, 127
Grass clippings – 18, 42, 66, 68, 78
Grass, Blue Oat – 27
Grass, Crab – 22, 72
Grasses, Blue – 21
  Nurse – 21
  Ornamental – 27
Grass, Quack – 22, 84
Gumbo – 11, 46, 51

H

Hardiness – 10, 27, 35, 36, 83-85, 117, 133
Heat, bottom – 28, 31, 96, 104, 119
Heather – 44
Hedges – 36, 51, 127
Hellebores – 10
Herbs – 11, 16, 30-40
Herbal remedies – 16, 38, 40
Herbicides – 18, 22, 23, 128
Herbicides, Non-selective – 23, 128

Heuchera – 8, 11
Heucherella – 8
Hoe – 52, 60, 70, 126
Hoe, chop – 52
Hoe, Dutch – 52
Hoe, scuffle – 52
Honeysuckle, Dropmore – 133
Hops – 133
Horehound – 35
Hoses – 19, 52, 78
Hosta – 10, 11, 12, 107
Houseplants – 54, 82, 86, 89, 90, 91, 94, 98, 109, 123
Hoya carnosa – 91
Humidity – 55, 84, 86, 92, 93, 99, 100, 102, 103, 104
Humus – 73, 78, 82, 84, 109, 119, 123
Hyacinth – 102, 122
Hyacinths, Grape – 113
Hybrid – 9, 16, 35, 36, 87, 106-109, 112, 118, 133
Hydrangeas, florist – 93
Hygiene – 55
Hyssop – 32, 33, 96

I

Impatiens – 96
Insecticidal soap – 23, 24, 34, 54, 58
Insects, scale – 90
Iris, German – 116, 117
  Japanese – 8, 116
  Siberian – 105, 116, 117
  Spanish – 117
Irrigation systems – 19, 131
Ivy, English – 110
Ixora coccinea – 82

J

Jasmine – 90
Joe Pye Weed – 12
Junipers – 134

K

Kiki – 87
Kozy Kote® – 71

L

Larkspur worm– 15, 54
Lavandin – 36
Lavender – 35, 36
Lawn, rolling – 20
Leaf cuttings – 97, 98
Leaf rollers – 58
Lettuce – 47, 73

Lettuce, Bitter – 73
Lettuce, Boston – 73
Lettuce, Iceberg – 73
Lettuce, leaf – 73
Lettuce, Romaine – 73
Lettuce, Summer Crisp – 73
Light, artificial – 76
Lilac – 11, 40, 55, 101, 110, 127, 128, 132
Lilies – 9, 16, 51, 58, 83, 88, 89, 90, 91, 102, 105, 123, 124
Lily, Calla – 90, 123, 124
Lily, Canna – 9, 105
Lily, Day – 16, 105
Lily, Easter – 83
Lily, Kafir – 91
Lily, Tiger – 102
Lily, Water – 51
Lipstick plants – 90
Loppers – 52, 127, 136
Lovage – 33, 40, 71
Lungwort – 11, 12, 105

M

Maggots, onion – 60
Mango – 109
Manure – 21, 34, 44, 45, 46, 48, 50, 51, 67, 68, 71, 74, 75, 78, 79, 110, 115, 119, 126, 129, 130
Manure, composted, 48, 78, 119, 130
Manure, green – 45, 48
Manure, pet – 48
Manure, tea – 75, 126
Manures, farmyard – 48
Marjoram – 37
Mealy bugs – 54, 64
Mildew – 19, 55, 72, 104
Mildew, Powdery – 19, 55
Mock Orange – 134
Moles – 59
Mosquitoes – 31, 56, 57
Mould, Snow– 19
Mulch – 10, 12, 18, 20, 26, 34, 66, 68, 69, 70, 74, 76, 77, 78, 79, 115, 116, 117, 129, 130
Mulch, plastic – 76
Mullein – 16
Murraya paniculata – 90
Muskmelons – 79
Mustard – 39, 70

N

Narcissus – 112, 114, 115
Nasturtiums – 54, 61, 71
Nicotine, Flowering – 14
Nitrogen – 18, 42, 43, 47, 48, 51, 68, 87, 88, 120, 129, 130
Nitrogen, slow-releasing – 18
No-Damp® – 96

O

Offsets – 78
Oil, cooking – 45, 54, 60, 126
Oil, Dormant – 60, 63, 127, 132
Onion maggots – 60
Onions – 15, 60, 70, 72, 73, 116, 120, 122
Orange, Calamondin – 94
Orchid Cactus – 88
Orchids – 50, 87
Orchids, Moth – 87
Oregano – 37, 60
Oregano, Cuban – 60
Organic material – 10, 46, 51, 68
Osmocote® – 129
Oxalic acid – 63, 71, 75
Oxygen – 42

P

Palms – 93, 123
Papaya – 109
Pasteurization – 50
Pear – 55, 101
Peas – 68, 76, 120
Peat Moss – 9, 12, 44, 46, 49, 50, 67, 84, 86, 90, 97, 99, 101, 103, 115, 119, 121, 123
Peat, Sphagnum – 49
Penstemons – 16
Peonies – 13, 105
Peperomia – 98
Peppers – 14, 76
Peppers, green – 14, 76
Perennials – 10, 11, 12, 13, 15, 16, 22, 27, 33, 37, 59, 72, 84, 88, 89, 105, 116, 120, 126, 130
Perennials, shade-loving – 11, 12
Perianth – 114, 115
Perlite® – 37, 49, 50, 87, 89, 90, 98, 101, 119
Pets – 22, 28, 42, 43, 48, 62
Petunias – 135
pH – 34, 44, 47, 67, 70, 79
Phalaenopsis – 87

Phlox – 55, 101, 116
Phlox, Arctic – 116
Phosphorus – 18, 21, 22, 25, 28, 40, 42, 47, 91, 112, 117, 120, 122, 123, 127, 132
Picotee – 118
Piggyback plant – 8
Pincushion Flowers – 16
Pine, Mugho – 135
Plum trees – 60
Poinsettia – 92
Poppy, Oriental – 101
Portulaca – 14
Potash – 47, 70, 123
Potassium – 18, 28, 47, 70, 77, 78, 86, 89, 91, 92, 94, 109, 123
Potatoes – 48, 67, 68, 103
Potatoes, certified seed – 67
Potato scab – 67
Prairie – 18, 24, 27, 28, 37, 46, 47, 57, 58, 61, 62, 67, 70, 83, 105, 128
Primrose, Evening – 14
Primrose, potted – 89
Primula – 83
Propagation – 11, 96, 99, 100, 101, 103, 107
Propagation, asexual – 96, 99, 107
Prune – 12, 51, 52, 106, 127, 128, 133, 134, 135
Pruners – 51
Pruners, Pole – 52
Pulmonaria – 11, 105
Pumpkins – 69, 77, 79, 80, 110
Pyrethrums – 24

Q

Quack Grass – 17, 22, 84

R

Rabbit's Foot Fern – 86, 100
Raccoons – 69
Radicchio – 74
Radishes – 73
Railway ties – 46
Raised beds – 46
Raspberries – 78, 127, 129
Reworking – 115, 127, 134, 135
Rhizomes – 9, 86, 117, 120
Rhododendrons – 44, 55
Rhubarb – 43, 48, 63, 71, 75, 105, 126
Root cutting – 101
Root divisions – 105
Rooting hormone – 37, 110

Rosemary – 38, 39
Roses – 40, 55, 56, 59, 101, 106, 110, 131, 135
Roses, bud union – 106
    Hybrid Tea – 106
Rotenone® – 15, 54, 63
Rototilling – 24, 44
Rudbeckia – 15, 16
Rue – 59
Runners – 12, 129
Rusts – 60
Ruta graveolens – 59

S

Sage – 37, 38
Sage, Bethlehem – 11
Salts, epsom – 66, 91
Sand – 20, 24, 45, 46, 51, 101, 102
Sanseveria trifasciata – 98
Satinwood – 90
Sawdust – 9, 46
Scab, potato – 67
Scabiosa –16
Scaling – 102
Scarecrows – 69
Scarlet Runner Beans – 12
Seaweed fertilizer – 78, 119, 128
Secateurs – 51, 52, 127, 136
Sedum – 98
Seed storage – 108
Seed versus sod – 21
Seed – 14, 21, 22, 24-26, 28, 31, 33, 34, 35, 37, 39, 40, 45, 66, 66-70, 73, 74, 76-79, 84, 85, 90, 96, 97, 103, 104, 107-110, 112, 129, 130, 131, 132
Seed, pre-germinate – 96
Seedling variation – 107
Seedlings – 26, 31, 90, 96, 103, 104, 107, 108, 129, 130
Shears – 51, 127, 134, 136
Skirting evergreens – 135
Skunks – 23
Slips – 99
Slow release fertilizers – 18, 42
Slug baits – 62
Slugs – 12, 61, 62, 77
Slugs, pear – 61
Snapdragons – 135
Snowdrop – 112
Sod webworm – 23
Sod – 21-25, 28, 59, 62
Soil, Alpine – 51

Soil, Composted – 12, 34, 42, 43, 44, 46, 48, 51, 61-63, 66-68, 71, 73, 74, 75, 77, 78, 79, 82, 86, 109, 110
Soil for Cactus – 51
Soil-wetting agent – 78, 128
Soil, Woodland – 10, 12
Sorrel – 32, 71
  French – 71
  Garden – 71
Spades, English – 45, 51
Spades, trenching – 51
Spirea – 134
Spider Mites – 54, 94
Spring tonics – 32, 75
Squash – 77, 79, 80
Squirrels – 58, 59
St. John's Wort – 16
Stakes – 15, 92, 126
Sterile mixes – 49, 50, 96, 98
Storage – 9, 15, 27, 30, 35, 52, 69, 88, 90, 96, 103, 105, 108, 110, 112, 120, 122-124, 129, 131
Strawberries – 70, 78, 129
Stump removal – 136
Suckers – 101, 128
Sugar content, corn – 69
Sulphur – 44, 55, 60, 67, 105, 127, 132
Sulphur, agricultural – 67
Sulphur, lime – 60, 127, 132
Summer Savory – 33
Sunflowers – 14
Sweet Peas – 97

T

Taro – 124
Tea, cold – 82, 84, 94
Tequila – 88
Terra cotta – 14, 38, 91, 124, 131
Thistles – 23, 130
Thrips – 63, 120
Thyme – 35
Tiarella – 11
Tomatoes – 14, 30, 61, 62, 66, 70, 132
Topdressing – 21, 22
Topiary – 36, 134
Triple Mix® – 26, 50
Trumpet – 85, 114, 115
Tubers – 67, 94, 103, 118, 120
Tulips – 112, 113, 114
Tulips, Double – 113
Tulips, Parrot – 113
2,4-D® – 23, 130, 136

U

USDA – 10, 93, 99, 115, 117, 123, 124

V

Valerian – 33, 40
Vermiculite – 49, 50, 90

W

Waterlilies – 51
Watermelons – 79
Weed killers – 15
Weeds – 15, 22, 23, 45, 46, 48, 52, 60, 70, 130
Weeds, perennial – 22, 130
Weeping Fig – 92
Weigela – 134
Whiteflies – 37, 54, 63, 83
Willow – 99
Wood ash – 70, 77
Worms – 24, 61
Wormwood – 33

Z

Zucchini – 77, 80
Zygocactus – 88, 107

SHARE TROWEL TIPS WITH A FRIEND

TROWEL TIPS ____ copies x $14.95 CDN/$12.95 US . . . . = $ _____

Shipping and handling (total order) . . . . = __4.00__

Subtotal . . . . = _____

In Canada add 7% GST (on book total + shipping) . . . . = _____

Total . . . . = $ _____

Method of payment: ☐ Cheque or Money Order enclosed ☐ VISA ☐ MasterCard

Card # _____   Exp. Date: _____

Signature: _____

Name: _____

Address: _____

City/Town: _____ Prov/State: _____ Postal/Zip _____

Phone: _____ Fax: _____

Please Make Checks, Money Orders or Inquiries to: Publishing Solutions
1150 Eighth Avenue
Regina, SK, Canada S4R 1C9

VISA/MasterCard orders: Fax 1-800-823-6829 or Phone Toll Free 1-800-667-5595
email: centax@printwest.com   www.centaxbooks.com

- -

SHARE TROWEL TIPS WITH A FRIEND

TROWEL TIPS ____ copies x $14.95 CDN/$12.95 US . . . . = $ _____

Shipping and handling (total order) . . . . = __4.00__

Subtotal . . . . = _____

In Canada add 7% GST (on book total + shipping) . . . . = _____

Total . . . . = $ _____

Method of payment: ☐ Cheque or Money Order enclosed ☐ VISA ☐ MasterCard

Card # _____   Exp. Date: _____

Signature: _____

Name: _____

Address: _____

City/Town: _____ Prov/State: _____ Postal/Zip _____

Phone: _____ Fax: _____

Please Make Checks, Money Orders or Inquiries to: Publishing Solutions
1150 Eighth Avenue
Regina, SK, Canada S4R 1C9

VISA/MasterCard orders: Fax 1-800-823-6829 or Phone Toll Free 1-800-667-5595
email: centax@printwest.com   www.centaxbooks.com